W9-CMQ-323

Patou

Patou

Meredith Etherington-Smith

St. Martin's / Marek
New York

To my father

PATOU. Text copyright © 1983 by Meredith Etherington-Smith.
Illustrations copyright © 1983 by the Patou Archive. All rights reserved.
Printed in the United States of America. No part of this book may be
used or reproduced in any manner whatsoever without written permission
except in the case of brief quotations embodied in critical articles or
reviews. For information, address St. Martin's/Marek , 175 Fifth Avenue,
New York, N.Y. 10010.

Library of Congress Cataloging in Publication Data

Etherington-Smith, Meredith.
    Patou.

    1. Patou, Jean, 1880-1936.   2. Costume designers—
France—Biography.   I. Title.
TT505.P37E84   1984   746.9′2′0924   [B]   84-13269
ISBN 0-312-59816-5 (pbk.)

First published in Great Britain in 1983 by Hutchinson & Co.
(Publishers) Ltd.

First U.S. Edition

10 9 8 7 6 5 4 3 2 1

Contents

Acknowledgements

The author would like to acknowledge the cooperation and encouragement shown to her in writing this biography on the part of Jean Patou's brother-in-law, M. Raymond Barbas, for many years President of the Chambre Syndicale de la Couture, without whose assistance and permission to utilize his splendid archives this book would never have been written. To his grandson, the present president of Patou, M. Jean de Mouy, grateful thanks for resolving many problems and for his active help from the beginning.

I am indebted to M. Barbas and M. de Mouy for permitting me to use many unique drawings and photographs from the Patou archive and from their private family albums. All such illustrations and photographs are Patou copyright.

I should also like to acknowledge and thank Condé Nast, publishers of *Vogue*, for permission to reproduce the illustrations on pages 8, 30, 35, 37 and 55, all of which are Condé Nast copyright.

To *Harper's Bazaar* my thanks for permission to reproduce the illustrations on pages 102, 117, 118, 119, 123, 132 and 135, all of which are copyright of the Hearst Corporation.

To Lillian Farley, known at the time as 'Dinarzade', grateful thanks for allowing me to read her memoirs and permission to quote from them in chapters 2 and 5. To Jonathan Hope, my thanks for some key research pointers.

Finally, my thanks to Celestine Dars for much invaluable picture research, both in Paris and London.

Introduction

If you turn off the rue de Rivoli, in Paris, just before you come to the Place de la Concorde, down a narrow little street called the rue St Florentin, you find on your left a large eighteenth-century *hôtel particulier* with one word incised into a brass plaque set into the side of the double carriage arch. The name is Patou.

And if you go through the arch, along the cobbled passageway of this building that once belonged to the French diplomat and opportunist, Talleyrand, and walk up the grey and beige main staircase to the first floor you might, as you ascend, almost be able to hear a low murmur. The sibilant rustle of cloche-hatted, straight-limbed fashionable ghosts. Dressed in neat, sprightly little *djersekasha* dresses, hatted in velours by Reboux, Marthe or Regnier, holding black antelope clutch bags, they would smell faintly of Que Sais-Je, Amour-Amour or Joy, the most potent scent of all.

These would be the spectres of the chic twenties clientele dressed by the couturier Jean Patou. They would, once again, be on their leisurely way up the grand staircase to one of his gala evening showings, biannual events on the social calendar of *le tout Paris.*

You might almost be able to catch the odd inquiry from the buzz of elegant conversation. What would Patou's new colour, rose-beige, be like? What would his theme be this season . . . shorter? Longer? Shades of Pola Negri, Mrs Harrison Williams and the Dolly Sisters, whispering to each other as they came at last into the three connecting salons on the first floor, might brush past.

A ghost from the future in this gathering, you emerge at the top of the stairs into the candlelit mirrored salons. Blond

7

and grey wood and cane chairs and
pale wood tables are arranged like a series of small desert
islands in a sea of beige carpet, reflected and refracted end-
lessly by enormous bevelled mirrors.

The house of Patou still presents exactly the same face to
its clients as it did in the twenties when the salons were first
designed for Jean Patou in the romantic (rather than the
cubist), art-deco manner by his friends the architect Louis
Sue and designer André Mare. Time has stood still and, even
today, you find yourself in a world that is essentially twenties.

It was in these salons that one of the most famous names
in Paris couture in the twenties practised what Edna, Mrs
Woolman Chase, then *Vogue*'s editor in chief, described as
'high art and heavy industry'. And it is in these glittering
rooms that one still feels, more pervasive than any scent he
blended, the presence of the most important ghost of all: the
presiding spirit of Jean Patou – suave and amused, theatrical,
shrewd but always enigmatic.

There is something curious about this sense of time
arrested, of ghosts not laid to rest. It is over forty years since

Patou died, and yet the name is as familiar as that of Chanel. The name today, however, is associated with the couture house and the scent – Joy, promoted as the most expensive scent in the world.

Even fashion historians know little more. They know Jean Patou existed, that he was a Paris couturier in the twenties, that he designed some amusing cubist sweaters and bathing suits and that he invented Joy.

It is extraordinary how little is known about one so influential and so famous in his time. It was principally Patou who turned early twenties boudoir beauties, suffering from an overdose of the Ballets Russes look, from languidly decorative love objects into energetic little sportswomen, and it was Patou, again, who turned them back into seductive sirens when the time was right: porcelain figurines dressed in slithery white satin sheaths.

Little that is tangible remains of the private Patou; his personality remains elusive. His work, personified by the art-deco splendour of his *maison de la couture*, is his monument and his *raison d'être*. There is only a memory of a man who enabled lissome sunburned twenties women to leapfrog on the beach in cubist bathing costumes made from jersey that he had tested, characteristically, to make sure it did not shrink – even in a hot bath.

9

Patou's appearance was striking. He was well over six foot, lean, with aquiline features, flat shining dark hair and luminous light grey eyes. Somewhat melancholy in repose, he had a mobile and expressive face. Typically Gallic with a volatile temper, Patou was often to be seen shaking with anger. These storms never lasted long, however, and afterwards he would laugh at himself.

He was painted at the height of his career (in 1924) in the white tie and tails that suited him so well by his friend DeNoyer de Segonzac and this portrait captures his innate elegance. The dapper appearance, the black and white of his hair and skin, seen at its best in strict evening clothes. He was, according to Elsa Maxwell, one of the most handsome men she had ever seen.

Every nuance, almost every lover, and every coromandel screen in Coco Chanel's life has been exhaustively explored, analysed and catalogued. But the spotlight of research has never been turned on her contemporary and arch-rival, Patou. All that is immediately apparent now is what he wished to be apparent during his lifetime, a sort of elegant façade constructed from the scent, the couture house and some charming *croquis* (fashion sketches). Behind the potent yet ephemeral image Patou has left behind of the driver of fast cars, the captain of Zouaves and the white-tied *homme de Paris*, there is little substance to flesh out the man.

The most obvious explanation for this dearth of information about Patou is that he died relatively young, at a time when his seemingly effortless, uncluttered clothes had been eclipsed by the more elaborate fantasies of the thirties: events which combined to cast the man behind those severe cubist dresses and sports clothes into obscurity and thus his posthumous reputation quickly faded too. Chanel had a difficult time in the thirties, but she made her comeback after the Second World War by reviving much of the less-is-more fashion philosophy that she – and Patou – had pursued so successfully in the twenties.

Almost half a century has blurred the fine, but distinct, differences easily apparent to their contemporaries between the work of these two designers. And yet it is to Chanel (partly, it must be said, by her own efforts) that much of the credit has been attributed for the work achieved by Patou at the zenith of his career in the mid-twenties in dressing the *garçonne*, the boy/girl amalgam that became the twenties *beau idéal*.

To begin to understand the nature of this elusive shadow and the reasons why his reputation faded is to demand an appreciation of the age in which Patou lived. Patou's career could not have flourished as it did at any other time or in any other place than Paris in the decade that began with the end of the First World War and which ended on 9 October 1929, the day Wall Street crashed.

Patou was more than a couturier with some fascinating clients, but certainly the broad spectrum of women he dressed reflects his almost universal appeal during the twenties. There was Suzanne Lenglen, the champion tennis player, and Elsie de Wolfe, doyenne of expatriate society in Paris in the twenties. There was Mona Harrison Williams, later the Countess Bismarck, who was always cited in the popular American press as one of the best-dressed women of her time, a view retrospectively endorsed by such fashionable contemporary chroniclers as Cecil Beaton and Van Dongen who painted her in Patou's black slipper satin petticoat chemise, with huge square-cut emeralds wound negligently round one of her celery-stick wrists.

Bringing these transatlantic members of high society together with Patou was the eccentric café-society clown Elsa Maxwell, who was not only a friend of Patou's but worked for him as social secretary during his most productive period, promoting his designs and, notably, Joy.

The demimonde of the stage also produced clients for Patou . . . the actress Geneviève Lantelme was an early client before her death by drowning off her lover's yacht, *L'Aimée*. The Dolly Sisters, who did absolutely everything together, including sharing their men and choosing their clothes at Patou, were clients both for their elaborate stage clothes and for the ensembles they wore so decoratively on the beaches and in the night clubs of smart society.

Patou also dressed quieter, more aristocratic ladies – among them the Princesse de Broglie, doyenne of Faubourg society, the Comtesse de Robillant, and English aristocrats such as Lady Diana Cooper, Lady Milbanke and Paula Gellibrand, who married the Marquis de Casa Maurey (known at the

time as the Cuban heel). Society weddings produced such
clients as Barbara Hutton, who wore a Patou gown of silk
satin for her first marriage to Alexei, one of those Georgian
princes christened 'the marrying Mdivanis' because that was
how they seemed to make their living.

Later, Patou was to dress Gloria Swanson *pour le sport*,
Mary Pickford in her delicate 'fluffy' dresses, and the darkly
dramatic German star Pola Negri (who married another Mdivani prince), both for her films and in her private life.

All these clients had something in common. They were
usually physically small and they had adventurous minds and
were energetic and independent. Patou confirmed his talent,
however, making 'difficult' customers, like the rather large
Elsa Maxwell, look well turned out too. He believed that
women should dominate their clothes rather than being couture clotheshorses, and that his business was to make as many
different types of women look as beautiful and as elegant as
possible. His fittings were always held by those in the know
to be the best in Paris.

So, like Hispano Suiza tourers, suntans, green hats, cubism,
jazz and the Riviera in summer, Patou was part of the bright
patchwork of new ideas, new people and a new, more modern
way of life that spelled the spirit of the twenties. He was
perhaps the personification of certain contemporary dreams,
aspirations and prevailing moods. His personality, with all its
faults, evasions and virtues, echoes the paradoxes of the jazz
age. He was immensely disciplined and at the same time
excessively volatile, a private man who wore a cleverly con-
trived public mask. A spendthrift and a brilliant businessman.
A ladies' man who loved no one woman and yet who preferred
to go shooting or fishing with his father and his brother-in-
law. A modernist with a strong sense of tradition.

The way Patou worked, the way he enjoyed himself, whom
he knew, precisely reflect certain glamorous aspects of the
twenties. The spirit of his age to the end, he survived it by
only six years.

An attempt to add substance to the shade of Patou in this
book, in order to re-establish him in the chronicles of
twentieth-century fashion, has led to a mystery, the roots of
which are to be found in his secretive personality. Accounts
of Patou's career and his private life vary enormously even

when obtained from the most reliable contemporary sources. Some, like the normally reliable Edna Woolman Chase, maintain that Patou was discovered almost overnight in about 1912, but the truth is that he had already been working as an independent tailor, furrier and then dressmaker for four years before that. An instance of just one discrepancy among many.

Most recent retrospective fashion exhibitions of the twenties have ignored Patou's work. In many indexes he does not appear at all, in other books he warrants only a footnote. Dates and details are vague, particularly in the early years, when he established Parry, his dressmaking and fur business at the Point Rond. Some accounts confuse this establishment with an earlier tailoring business which went bankrupt. The explanation for all this may be Patou's own evasiveness concerning dates, and since he did not score an instant success in his first years he may, rather like Chanel, have chosen to be airily imprecise about records.

One feels that Patou deliberately led his public life in the spotlight of high society and journalism, but that behind this beautifully manufactured façade of smart parties, and heavy and well-publicized gambling, there was another, quieter existence with its roots firmly in his past and with his family. His mother, his father, his sister Madeleine whom he adored, his brother-in-law Raymond Barbas, were all part of a more bourgeois life, far from the glitter of the Riviera and the rue St Florentin. Here he was the dutiful son and the devoted brother, and it is probable that this quiet family life provided such emotional completeness that he never felt the need to create a family of his own.

Patou guarded this privacy so zealously that it remains a mystery today. Those few who were privileged to know the private Patou still, after fifty years, retain their guard at this closed door. Although often the focus of society's interest in his prime, little of Patou remains now beyond some faded newspaper clippings, a few people who remember (though not many) and occasional mentions in contemporary autobiographies.

Patou's relationships with women are noteworthy for their variety and number, but no hint of a permanent attachment to any one woman is left to us. He appeared to love many

. . . for a moment. He is thought to have had brief liaisons with hundreds of the young seamstresses or *grisettes* who filled his workrooms but such dalliances, surprisingly, were not the stuff of gossip and thus go unrecorded. No single woman managed to have a deep relationship with Patou or one that transcended brief public or social appearances. The nearest he ever came to permanence was apparently with the Grand Duchess Marie of Russia – there were rumours of marriage in 1925 – but this is the only time the press ever mentioned Patou in the context of marriage. He was one of the most confirmed bachelors in Paris, at a time when the phrase was emphatically not a euphemism for homosexuality.

One reason for the decline of Jean Patou's reputation is simple: the clothes by eminent designers that are given to museums are often not the favourite, well-worn dresses, but ones that were bought for a special occasion, or worn only once. The essence of a Patou design, however, was that it was so beautifully cut and the workmanship so exquisite that you lived in it until it wore out. With the exception of his wedding dresses and some of the more elaborate solidly sequinned evening gowns, Patou's clothes were made for real life, made to wear and wear again, not for show.

A second explanation for Patou's present obscurity perhaps lies in the fact that he was in financial low water when he died: his business, turning over more than today's equivalent of £5 million a year in the mid-twenties, was, by the mid-thirties, subsisting on the revenue brought in by the perfumes he had created, and by dressmaking for the few private clients who had remained faithful to him. He had disappeared from the public eye although his death revived his name for a time. His successors, his sister Madeleine and his brother-in-law Raymond Barbas, while keeping alive the tradition of exquisite workmanship and fittings established by Patou, decided to turn 'Jean Patou' into a generic label, rather than emphasizing the man himself, in order to instil confidence in the business once again. Thus a man became an industry.

The reason for these financial reversals is not hard to find. Elsa Maxwell put it succinctly in her autobiography, *R.S.V.P.* 'It is safe to say that Patou wagered and lost more money in the casinos of France and Monte Carlo than any gambler in

14

history.' Her explanation of this behaviour was that his experience as an infantryman and later as a captain in the Zouaves during the First World War had left him stamped with an 'indelible imprint of recklessness'.

The shrewd businessman, therefore, was also one of Europe's most determined playboys. The fortune he earned as a couturier in the twenties was spent on women, parties, cars, gambling, fast boats and lavishly decorated houses. The First World War changed Patou from a conscientiously careful member of the French middle class into a man who only felt alive when he was risking everything. Having seen many of his friends killed in front of him, he could never form lasting and satisfying personal relationships with anyone but the members of his own family. He came back from the fighting with lasting emotional problems.

In the end, this recklessness, combined with the economic problems created for couture by the Wall Street crash, the changing taste of the thirties (to which he proved less than sensitive), conspired to make Patou's last few years difficult.

The third explanation for the almost total eclipse of Patou's reputation as a designer is that he died long before the time was right to make a comeback with the simple, subtle glamour that was his trademark. When women were once again ready for rigorous simplicity and understated elegance in the mid-fifties, when the mood of the times was buoyant again, it was the great survivor Chanel who was the phoenix. The fashionable world was then once again confident enough to be casual and unadorned; Chanel's 'nothing' clothes echoed a new freedom and lightness of spirit.

Patou was a vital and fascinating man, perhaps schizophrenic in the absolute division between his public and private lives, but living in feverish times when irrationality was perceived by some as an integral part of the creative impulse. He was part of a world of energy and seemingly limitless possibilities, in which Paris was the magnet for most who aspired to elegance, taste, intellectual pursuit.

Patou was once asked what he thought would be fashionable in the future. 'Fashion is not a subject of deduction, like a system of logic,' he replied. 'It is made up of a thousand different influences. Fashion is a living thing and, in consequence, evolves from day to day, from hour to hour and from minute to minute.' Jean Patou's minute spanned a decade. The man and his age were made for, and in terms of fashion by, each other. All the faults, follies, triumphs, tribulations and fun of the twenties were essentially those of Patou as well.

He liked and understood the 'new woman' and dressed her as a real person rather than as a plaything. 'Women are not dolls to be dressed by designers,' he said, but in his private life he treated women as dolls that could indeed always be exchanged for a newer, prettier version. 'I would ask them, have you no brains? Yes, you have intelligence. Then please express that intelligence in dressing yourself.' But the only woman whose intelligence he trusted was his sister Madeleine.

'To be modern does not mean to upset and revolutionize,' said Patou, who was himself later to revolutionize the entire fashion industry by being the first to drop hemlines. 'A modern style is not a style which forgets all tradition of the past and from day to day pretends to impose a new rule. To be modern is to have the thought, the tastes and the instincts of the epoch in which one lives.' In this, both sides of his personality unite. 'We are witnessing a renaissance and, because of this, harmony is not yet complete among the various parts of the society in which we live where, in consequence of new inventions, certain elements have developed faster than others.' He might have been using his description of the age in which he lived as a metaphor for his own contradictory personality.

Jean Patou understood his age, if not himself.

1

The Zouave

Jean Patou was born in Normandy in 1880, with many advantages for one who was later to make his fortune as a leading arbiter of taste in dress.

He was the eldest of the two children of Charles and Jeanne Patou. It must have been a close and happy family, for all his life, even at the height of his social success in the 1920s, Patou would sometimes go fishing at Duisy, outside Paris, with his father and his brother-in-law. He was seven years older than his sister Madeleine, but always very close to her, finding in her neat elegance the inspiration for much in his designs. The two children had the sort of secure family life that Proust describes at the beginning of *A la Recherche du Temps Perdu*. It was prosperous, bourgeois and comfortable.

Money was plentiful, for Patou's father, Charles, was one of France's leading tanners in the late nineteenth century. Jeanne's family, the Grisons, had been prosperous leather tanners for three generations, and Patou's father ran the business, specializing in the tanning of the very finest leathers which were used mainly for bookbinding. These fine-grained sealskins, moroccos and aniline calf leathers were tanned in the most subtle colours, for Charles Patou had flair in the refined art of dyeing. His superb colour sense found its expression in dyeing leathers for the art of rare bookbinding which became very popular in the 1880s and 1890s, largely as a result of the influence of the arts and crafts movement.

This was the time when patrons such as the couturier Jacques Doucet commissioned the most exquisite bindings for their books, and the art flourished as it had not done since the French Revolution a hundred years earlier. Jean Patou's eye for colour at its most evanescent, its most subtle, was undoubtedly inherited from his father, and it was to contribute greatly to his success as a couturier.

Patou invariably introduced a new colour each season; it was always exclusively his, and he worked with fabric suppliers such as Bianchini Ferier and Rodier to create such tints as 'Dark Dahlia' introduced in 1929 and the famous 'Patou Blue' in 1923. This was a deep, sky blue with subtle violet undertones, giving a transient surface effect to any fabric dyed with it. It was a triumph of the colourist's art – and Patou frequently returned to it, either as a solid colour, or in combination with new tones. He often used it with white in the summer to create a sparkling sporty effect, and it was particularly pretty when worked into his simple cubist sweaters. The other blue that Patou loved was a dark, almost black, navy, and the navy and white combination he returned to again and again throughout the twenties became a uniform for smart women who felt that Chanel's beige was drab. In the twenties, when for most designers anything went as long as it was beige or possibly black, Patou never abandoned colour and brightness.

He was expected to follow his father into the family business, but this plan went badly awry when he was faced with the everyday realities of tanning. Even in his teens, Patou showed signs of the exquisite he was later to become, and the apprenticeship his father insisted upon did not suit his inclinations. 'I had to spend my days in filthy mud,' he said. 'Had I remained in my father's leather business, I should never have got on in life.'

Years later, talking in an uncharacteristically frank way to the photographer Baron de Meyer, Patou justified what must have been a matter of deep distress to his family at the time, this abandonment of the family business 'We Frenchmen are good businessmen,' he told de Meyer, 'as good as any others, only we are hampered by tradition and it prevents individual development. Sons are always supposed to enter their father's business. They start young, are full of enthusiasm and new ideas, but are not permitted to give expression to any of them, such views being systematically stifled by the father.

'My father disgusted me with his business, and instead of following in his wake, I joined an uncle of mine [in 1907] who dealt in furs.' The resulting family quarrels can only be imagined, but when Patou went to war in 1914 – by then a successful independent dressmaker – all acrimony was forgotten.

Patou's work as a furrier did not last very long, for early in his career with his uncle he realized that furriers were at a disadvantage. Truly wealthy customers often preferred buying furs from their couturiers, such as the all-powerful Englishman, Worth, finding it more convenient and the furs themselves often more stylish.

Patou acted decisively. 'I began to plan an establishment of my own; dressmaking combined with furs.' This first venture, started in 1910, foundered for reasons which he subsequently glossed over as 'needless to record' – no doubt unfortunate for his financial backers, probably his relatives. 'But it taught me dressmaking,' said Patou.

Patou started again, opening a tailoring business in 1911 which fared better, and which he eventually sold in preparation for his third venture. This time, in 1912, he combined tailoring, dressmaking and furs, offering the same services, on a more modest level, that the smart Parisian would then have expected from a couturier.

What this young man who was to make his name designing clothes of a rigorous *sportif* simplicity thought of all the rather humid boudoir dressing of the first decade of the twentieth century can only be surmised. Did he plan, as he sat cutting and draping the exquisitely airy lace flounces or hobble skirts his prewar customers demanded, how he was going to take the rue de la Paix, then the centre of Paris couture, by storm one day with some new way of dressing that would make women look and feel like living, active people, rather than immobile, constricted lace bolsters?

The woman that Patou was to dress – and upon whom he made his name – did not yet exist. She was born as a direct result of the social changes emerging in the First World War. She was to be freer, more independent, and no longer prepared to be constricted by her clothes. She would wish to feel a new spirit of liberation and a way of dressing to echo her mood. She would, of course, be rich, but her style and her unconscious demand for clothes would nevertheless personify her new freedom.

In the meantime, in the world of the *belle époque* there were two careers open to women of wealth or women who wished to acquire wealth: to be married or to be a coquette. Women were kept, and fashion reflected this by turning women into walking, or rather hobbling, displays of male wealth. The huge cartwheel hats, the elaborate and constricting busked lace gowns, the glaciers of diamonds, ropes of pearls all added up to woman as helpless love objects. The only women who were free in this dying world were a few very successful demimondaines, the *grandes horizontales* such as Emilienne d'Alençon, who often wore mannish *tailleurs*, and Cléo de Mérode, the fiery Spanish dancer.

In 1912, when Patou opened his first demicouture establishment in Paris, Maison Parry, the liberated woman and the new way she would dress still lay beyond the cataclysm of the war.

Maison Parry, while having no pretensions to being a leading couture house, able to influence fashion direction, none the less did dress a fair number of actresses and demimondaines, such as the beautiful red-headed Geneviève Lantelme, the mistress of newspaper proprietor Alfred Edwards, married to Misia Sert. Dressmaking establishments such as Parry fulfilled other useful functions in the louche first decade of the century, in that they could be used as romantic meeting places, the discreetly curtained fitting rooms providing many opportunities for quiet romantic meetings. Hearing one afternoon that the notoriously fickle La Lantelme had such an assignation at Maison Parry, Alfred Edwards attempted to catch her *in flagrante delicto* and was astonished to find her being fitted for a new chinchilla coat.

'I am a lucky man,' Patou said in 1923, of his success with Maison Parry.

Firstly, had I known when I opened my first dressmaking establishment what I know now, it would have remained closed for ever. Clothes, fashions in general, were a sealed book to me. I knew nothing about them, especially not in the days of rigid fashion discipline and uniformity of styles distinct from season to season. Had I known my business at that time I would have been aware that long coats were *de rigueur* that year, instead of which I disregarded tradition and in sheer ignorance showed a collection composed exclusively of short jackets.

American buyers who had evidently come to patronize a debutant's efforts were surprised that I should show short coats instead of the universally adopted long ones. They proclaimed me a daring innovator and I was voted a success . . . don't you call that luck?

Nevertheless, it might have seemed as if his luck had run out in the early days. The simplicity he preferred, which depended on very complicated cutting to give a 'nothing' effect, was difficult for clients, who were used to tucking, draping and waterfalls of lace, to understand. Patou did not toe the rue de la Paix line established by the grander couturiers such as Worth and Doucet, yet nor was he as controversial as Poiret then was.

Patou's line was essentially neat, a word to be associated for ever with the couturier. He balanced the fashionable higher waist, columnar draping and ankle-length skirt with late-*Directoire* fichus and tucked sleeves. His long skirts were slightly hobbled and cut short to the ankle, revealing clever little elastic-sided boots.

By 1914 Patou was beginning to develop the precision of cut that in the twenties, the years of his success, was the hallmark of every dress, coat or jacket that left his house. He had begun to work using inset godets, panels and the concealed pleating that became his design signature. Simplicity started to pay off and early Patou clients included some well-known names such as the Comédie Française actress Alyx who, among other professional beauties, wanted something less recognizable than Poiret's oriental fantasies, and something less expensive.

From 1912, when he launched his Minaret collection, Poiret had dominated Paris couture. A man of titanic energy and unsurpassed showmanship, he had single-handedly released women from corsets – only to introduce a new area of constriction, the ankle. His women wore oriental-style clothes partly inspired by Bakst's designs for the Ballets Russes and partly by Poiret's own researches into Persian miniatures. One of fashion's recurrent oriental revivals once again swept Paris as it had done many times before (and has done since), notably in the mid-eighteenth century when the chinoiserie craze took hold.

Poiret's skirts were severely hobbled at the ankle, his waists were high under the bust, and his colours about as far removed, in their primitive violence, from Doucet or Worth's gentle sweet-pea tones as could be imagined.

He commissioned the artist Georges Lepape to produce an exquisite limited edition portfolio of his collection called *Les Choses de Paul Poiret*. It was sensational. Poiret's name thus spread far beyond the boundaries of Paris couture. His enormous success and the continuing popularity of more classical couture left Patou's simpler designs in a no-man's-land: and the all-important Seventh Avenue retailers, who spent enormous sums buying models to copy and sell in America, stayed away. Patou became, unusually for him, despondent and began to wonder, as he confided years later to Edna Woolman Chase, whether he had chosen the wrong métier.

The New York Seventh Avenue retailers played an important part in the history of couture in the early years of the twentieth century. They were the vital link between the couturiers and the increasing number of women in America who, without actually being able to go there and undergo expensive and time-consuming fittings in one of the couture houses, wanted a dress 'from Paris'.

These sharp-eyed buyers, such as Hattie Carnegie, came to the collections and afterwards purchased models which would then be copied in the workrooms of New York, often in identical fabrics. Buyers came too from England, Italy and Spain to choose models, and, as the twenties progressed, what was designed for the private client and what was designed with mass production in mind diverged. Patou, for instance, always added several 'quiet' numbers to his collection after the buyers went home, intended solely for his private clients, such as the American Mrs Scudamore, who wanted subtle refinement rather than blatant trendsetting.

Competition between these buyers was fierce and many of them were not above purchasing only one or two models and then copying the rest of the collection from memory. By the mid-twenties the couturiers had caught on to this, and led by Madeleine Vionnet they registered all their models by photographs kept as a record, establishing a kind of patent. There was also a buyers' black list, always headed by the Germans who were evidently notorious copyists.

The Seventh Avenue buyers were the financial force that eventually changed couture from being a group of small businesses dedicated to the dressing of rich private clients in virtually one-off designs, into an industry which directly or indirectly clothed, perfumed and 'painted' women from New York to Tokyo.

In 1913 confirmation of Patou's talent at last arrived in the unlikely shape of a Seventh Avenue buyer known as the elder Lichtenstein. Arriving at Maison Parry unannounced to buy two or possibly three winter models, he bought the entire collection outright, presaging Patou's enormous future success in America, where, once he had established a foothold, he flourished well into the thirties.

Patou's designs in 1913 were much like others of the period, if a little simpler. The whalebones, drapes and flounces of the *belle époque* had begun to recede, leaving behind a legacy of lighter clothes of a cobweb delicacy and prettiness from Doucet and Callot Soeurs. Lace was still used, but it was cut much more simply and prettily. Patou's line, judging by the meagre records that survive, is less obsessed with oriental detailing and is more realistic, purer in mood.

The main inspiration for Patou at this time and indeed throughout his career was his enchanting sister Madeleine. Contemporary photographs show her dressed in mannish serge two-pieces with frogged trimming, giving her a slightly military air. The war was a year away and, uncannily, fashion, as it sometimes does, reflected future developments before they occurred. Patou was always very much in tune with this curious fashion ESP.

Madeleine, who had inherited her dark hair and eyes from her mother, was classically beautiful and had the 'neat' quality that Patou so admired. She was, in fact, the perfect 'Patou' woman in her small build and physical precision. Madeleine's influence on her brother's career extended beyond his design inspiration, for when she married (in 1920) she brought her husband Raymond Barbas into her brother's business. She played a shadowy role in the business during the twenties. Busy bringing up her daughter Sylvie, who herself was later to run part of the Patou empire for a time, and whose son Jean de Mouy is the current director of the enterprise, Madeleine acted as Patou's confidante and, with her husband's restraining influence, managed to curb some of her brother's excesses. Madame Barbas was a byword for elegance, and

she had great common sense when it came to influencing decisions in the enormous industry that Maison Patou had become by the end of the twenties. However, Madeleine was disinclined to take more than a backstage role in the business, leaving the centre of the stage to her brother.

Raymond Barbas is probably one of the very few people who knew the real Patou behind the brilliant public image. He joined his brother-in-law's business the year after it started and he has been inextricably entangled in its fortunes ever since. It is through the eyes of this former champion tennis player that we have the clearest picture of the paradoxical Patou. It was thanks to Raymond Barbas that Patou became aware of a vital element in the smart life of the twenties and one which was to help him enormously in making his name – sport.

A member of the French national tennis team in the twenties, Barbas knew most of the leading sportsmen and women of his day, and for Patou, hitherto more accustomed to dining at Maxim's or Ciro's than to watching a tennis match, an interest in competitive sport and an understanding of its demands was to become one of the foundation stones of his success.

Patou believed he was lucky and recalled his good fortune in the timing of his first collection as a fully fledged couturier – although to anyone less optimistic, what he termed luck might be called a malign stroke of fate. 'Having planned to open my present establishment in the rue St Florentin on 1 August 1914,' he told Baron de Meyer, 'I was compelled to report at Nancy two days earlier, disguised as a second lieutenant of the Zouaves, ready to march. I left my completed collection behind me, and four years later, on seeing it again,' he commented, 'I realized my luck. For had I shown it then, it would surely have proved to be a phenomenal failure.'

Patou was careful to leave no records of this first collection: perhaps he destroyed them deliberately? Interestingly, he kept records of every collection he designed after the First World War.

Divergence from the standard fashion direction notwithstanding, Patou had finally decided in March 1914, just before the war, that Maison Parry had been successful enough to

25

warrant a major move against the entrenched couturiers of the rue de la Paix. He would open his own couture house.

In 1914 Patou decided to take the whole of the *hôtel parti-culier* at 7 rue St Florentin. It offered him the possibility of making just such a grand gesture that he would always enjoy. 'My brother-in-law was never a man who did things by halves,' says Raymond Barbas, 'and he opened a complete couture house; dressmaking, tailoring and furs.'

The house already had an interesting past, having been acquired by the eighteenth-century opportunist Talleyrand as a convenient home for his mistress, Adeline, Comtesse de Flahaut. Opposite the Hôtel Talleyrand, the house passed to Talleyrand's niece Dorothea, Duchess of Dino, on the second marriage of Mme de Flahaut.

By the turn of the century, it had become a rundown warren of small and large apartments. The simplicity of the eighteenth-century structure had not been completely de-stroyed, however, and the huge interlocking state reception rooms on the first floor were perfect for Patou. It was large, it could be grand again, it was near the rue de la Paix and close to the Ritz. As a couture house, it could not have been better planned. Where eighteenth-century footmen and maids slept in the attics, Patou housed his army of *grisettes*, the sewing girls, backbone of the couture industry, who worked at long horseshoe-shaped tables.

The stage was set for his first collection, but instead of becoming the youngest couturier in Paris, Patou volunteered and found himself en route to Nancy, the Zouaves and the war. He was not to see Paris again until 1919. The smart little streets of the Right Bank were exchanged for tiny peas-ant villages in Anatolia, and occasional leaves spent by the Bosporus.

These five years put an end to his old life almost as finally as if he had died like so many of his fellow countrymen. Patou went to the war as a man entrenched in the late nineteenth century and he returned reborn as a twentieth-century modernist.

He was well aware of the effect that five years' deprivation and constant danger had had on him. 'I went to the war like thousands of other Frenchmen, an ardent patriot, rather re-actionary, but with little knowledge of my compatriots of the lower classes,' he told a friend afterwards. He came back with changed ideas about life and work and with a new understanding of working people.

The mentality and the surprising natural intelligence of the men in my regiment, mostly peasants and small farmers, conquered me absolutely. Their behaviour was admirable. Their common sense in all matters and their warm heartedness were of a kind I had never come across in my own class, much less so among my former associates of Ciro's and Maxim's.

The Zouaves were crack troops and Patou had been a reservist in the regiment before the war. He found himself fighting in a small platoon which travelled fast towards the enemy, making daring sallies and retreats. There were no lines as such, no massive advances by whole regiments. Individual bravery as well as the camaraderie of very different men, united under their officers, counted for less than teamwork. Patou came back from the First World War as a captain, with a deep understanding of human motivation and this he applied in his relations with his work force.

The war has taught me that a certain amount of independence given to one's assistants is essential. Most *chefs de maison* hold contrary views, but it is my conviction that a modern business enterprise should be modelled on the lines of an army organization. The chief must give his orders, but he must not be expected to bother about the execution of details. He should be free to consider new ideas and submit them to his staff after his first orders have been carried out. If the person whose business it is to create and have ideas must also attend to their execution, he will be doomed to failure, for instead of remaining chief of the organization, he assumes the role of superintendent.

The lessons in commanding men Patou had learned in this dreadful school endured and in business he always remembered to delegate. Delegation left him free to explore the new ideas and cultural influences in Paris in the twenties, making him acutely sensitive to changing moods.

Patou was intrigued by new ideas wherever he found them and Paris after the war was a perfect hunting-ground for new attitudes, new art, architecture and design. Delegation also

27

meant that he was able to spend far more time on such matters as research into the development of new colours and fabrics, rather than simply accepting what was on offer from manufacturers. The constant search for the fresh and the special and the original ideas he developed with companies such as Rodier gave Patou clothes a distinction and an unmistakably original vision.

If Patou learned how to be a true *patron* while he was fighting, he also learned a rather more sinister lesson. He acquired his taste for danger, and not only to welcome it when it occurred, but to encourage it with a certain recklessness. Living on the knife edge became as addictive as a drug for Patou and he fed this addiction with feverish gambling, both at the tables in Biarritz and Monte Carlo, and eventually in his business as well. The pressures of the war created an imbalance in Patou's character from which he was never to recover.

His only stability was his private family life. It seemed all he needed, or indeed could cope with, and his business in a sense provided him not just with a fabulous amount of money with which to indulge in expensive distractions but also with a kind of emotional outlet as well.

If the war had changed Patou for ever, the Paris that he returned to in 1919 had also changed. The couture business had undergone an upheaval; among other things the old clientele had virtually vanished. It was on this altered landscape that Patou now ventured to establish his name and build up his business.

2

7 · rue St Florentin

Patou returned to a Paris which was almost unrecognizable. And yet he was faced with a fight for professional survival in this unfamiliar city every bit as real as his fight for personal survival in the last five years. The couture business had virtually ceased during the war. Paul Poiret spent those years designing and making army uniforms instead of oriental fantasies. The great houses of Worth, Doucet, Paquin, Callot Soeurs and Drécoll managed to dress their private clients as best they might with staff too old to fight or to work in the munitions factories. Patou, however, had gone to war, but such had been his faith in his work he had retained his small staff during the war years.

Patou's financial situation was now grave: for an established couturier to keep on his staff would not have been such a rash decision, but to Patou, funded only by the profits he had made from Parry, matters were desperate, even though the key staff in a couture house at that time were very few: the *première*, who translated ideas into finished clothes, the chief *modellistes*, who made the first samples, probably at that stage in Patou's career numbering one or two, and the accountant.

Seamstresses and fitters had to be employed, but they had always been paid a very low basic wage, making up their money to subsistence level by working overtime before and just after a collection was shown. It must have been extremely worrying, even to the optimistic Patou, to contemplate the inroads into his capital being made by keeping his couture house in readiness for his return from a tent in the middle of Anatolia.

He came back with another reminder of his time in the

Zouaves: his batman, Georges Bernard who, for the remaining seventeen years of Patou's life, was to play an important supporting role both privately and professionally. Bernard looked after his *patron* as effectively as he had taken care of the captain of Zouaves, in this role smoothing over ruffled feelings, organizing parties and diplomatically dealing with Patou's increasingly complicated social arrangements. His title of *directeur* covered a multitude of tasks.

Most of Patou's prewar clients had defected to tailors, to other couturiers and dressmakers, and many of them had already hitched their wagon to Chanel's rising star, whose career, far from being interrupted by the war, had prospered from it. Patou's fabric suppliers had nothing to offer him in the way of fantasy fabrics. Plain stuff, if you could get it, was the order of the day. And yet, fashion direction was diffused, and to every couturier this presented a major problem. The spring collections of 1919 had shown a bewildering variety of looks, most of them harking back to prewar trends with a few minor modifications, despite earlier signs of innovation.

There were the remnants of the Poiret minaret look, the only development from his prewar versions being a slight shortening of skirts to just above their prewar ankle length. There was also a more youthful ingénue look, the 'Dolly Varden' shepherdess dresses of figured and embroidered organdies and stiffened bell-like skirts reminiscent of the 1830s. This shape was also clumsily carried through to heavy mannish costumes in stiff serges and flannels. There was a *Directoire* look too, featuring military froggings and braid, trimming coats with huge stiff collars, big turned-back cuffs and lots of large buttons.

As soon as he had been demobilized, Patou plunged into the rebuilding of his atrophied business with gusto. 'He was an instant success, really,' says Raymond Barbas, 'because you must realize that the life we were all leading began to be led on a very big scale again, almost immediately the war had finished. At that time there were two or three young designers competing with the old ones like Poiret and Worth. The younger generation were led by my brother-in-law and Coco Chanel.'

Of the two young couturiers, Chanel tended to dress the more intellectual members of this new society and those of

the old guard with careful pretensions to modernity. Patou claimed the international café society good sports. His women moved! They travelled in fast cars, moving from the Riviera in summer to St Moritz in the winter. They divided their time between Paris, New York and chic holidays. They were often American, South American or they could be truly Parisienne, but they were always adventurous, with notions of being sporty or at least looking as if they played tennis or golf, even if they didn't. They were international and, even if funded by new money, they appreciated workmanship, fittings and subtle elegance.

The atmosphere in Paris became frenetic, and one curious reaction to the war was the enormous popularity in Paris of fancy-dress balls with correspondingly fantastic costumes worn with violet, jade green, orange and bright yellow wigs. The fashionable young began to talk of *un grog* in preference to *un aperitif* under the influence of American and English troops on leave, and the word 'crazy' became a popular catchphrase to describe almost anyone with any sense of style. These were the diverse influences that Patou had to interpret for his fashion-conscious clients.

Fresh air was beginning to blow through the boudoirs and the salons and much of it had come from America. In 1917, for instance, the first real signs that far-reaching changes were on the way (changes that would affect Patou in common with every other couturier) appeared in the taut, lithe form of a ballroom dancer, Mrs Vernon Castle. She was as light as a puff of air, as insubstantial as a moth and seemed to move in an entirely new way, 'turning against the way she was moving as if she had a hidden gyroscope built in,' as Cecil Beaton put it. Her effect of lightness and grace, of vibrant life and health, was augmented by her ethereal slimness. 'You could almost see the muscles under her skin ripple,' said Beaton. She was the direct opposite of the mature figure fashionable immediately before the war, and she captivated Paris with new dances such as the maxixse and the bunny hug with her partner and husband Vernon. Suddenly other women longed for her lissome energy. She was the first tangible sign that a new, idealized woman might be emerging.

'A style is often a faithful representation of the epoch in

31

which it was conceived,' Patou was to tell journalists in the mid-twenties.

The slow-moving prewar era sponsored trailing, clinging draperies and showy trimmings, all features suggesting wealth and leisure. The woman who wore such clothes seldom walked, and if she did, it was with great majesty and dignity.

Today a couturier's task is not so easy. He cannot satisfy himself or his clients with merely 'dressing' them. The life of a modern woman is a hurried, fast-moving one. The creator must therefore clothe her in consequence and make the best of the most simple of means to retain her feminine appearance and charm.

The fashions of today are indicative of a new and changed way of living, at any rate so far as a woman's evening activities are concerned. Formal entertainment at home is slowly being resumed, hence the return of the train and the sumptuous note present in all evening and some day clothes. There are clothes today that clearly define every hour of the day for the woman of leisure, but faithful to the new tradition, the couturier will never attempt to hamper her liberty of movement.

Paris society began to be more public, moving away from the nineteenth-century enclosed and private world of the Proustian Faubourg salons, their presiding spirits the great hostesses such as Mme Greffulhe, dressed by Worth. For years foreigners, and indeed foreign ideas, had scarcely penetrated these strongholds of French aristocracy. After the war the salons of the Faubourgs looked a little dusty in the harsh glare of electric light, and it was more amusing to go and listen to 'jazz', the exciting new import from America. As the *nouveaux riches* came into circulation, so society became more outward looking, welcoming into almost all its inner strongholds professional ballroom dancers, war profiteers, monied South Americans, rich Americans such as Winnaretta Singer, Princesse de Polignac, Nathalie Barney, Gertrude Stein, as well as the Castles, and White Russians fleeing the revolution. Poorer Americans fleeing the restrictions of the Midwest were welcome if they were talented or interesting. It was the beginning of postwar international café society, and Patou was one of its leading figures, both socially and professionally.

After the Armistice and the Peace Conference at Versailles, Paris began to consolidate its position as the centre of fun and frivolity, of new movements in art, of a rejuvenation in intellectual and social life. But there were many frayed and missing threads in this busy tapestry. The war had swept away the dominating position in Paris society of the great Faubourg hostesses: many of their men had died at the front and their position of social and cultural supremacy, unrivalled since the days of the First Empire, was being besieged from without and undermined from within.

Before the war, leaders of smart Parisian society had been the traditional *gratin* (literally, the big cheese): they were the pre-revolutionary aristocrats, those with Napoleonic titles, and the new money of the Second and Third Empires that had by then become established. These formidable women were the patronesses of the established rue de la Paix couturiers. Their fallen sisters, the *grandes horizontales*, also patronized the couturiers, but they had also been prepared to venture into newer fields, such as Maison Parry. Nevertheless, smart Paris and the couture houses that catered for it had been ruled essentially by old money until the First World War.

Paris had become more than just a social and fashion centre in the years immediately before the war. It had already attracted painters and writers from all over the world to its ateliers, cheap rooms, and to its dynamic atmosphere – the centre of modernist movements. Artistic and music salons and literary enclaves sprung up around these émigrés and their wealthy international patrons – Gertrude Stein and Alice B. Toklas in the rue de Fleuris; Misia Sert, that cultural gadfly and invaluable link between the worlds of music, ballet, art, literature and those with the money to patronize them; Winnaretta Singer, Princesse de Polignac whose music salon attracted the most avant garde of her time; Peggy Guggenheim, Harry and Caresse Crosby, Sarah and Gerald Murphy. They came and, after the war, stayed on to become the new patrons of such essentially Faubourg concerns as culture and couture.

A new sort of link had been forged between the worlds of art, music, literature and fashion, which had not really mixed much or influenced each other since the days of the First Empire. This link was provided by that Svengali of talent, Diaghilev, whose particular forte was commissioning diverse talents to design, score and choreograph ballets. The resulting energy and ideas affected fashion and had done so since Poiret was influenced by Bakst's designs for Diaghilev's ballet *Scheherezade* before the war.

The strident designs of post-Impressionist painters such as Matisse, Cubists such as Braque and the more romantic work of Raoul Dufy were enormously influential in the development of a relationship between artistic movements and fashion that has not been equalled since. For instance, Dufy was employed by Paul Poiret to design special prints which were then executed by Bianchini Ferier and are regarded as classics of their kind.

This crossfertilization of art and fashion and society grew more and more important to the couture business during the twenties, with some startling results, notably in Patou's cubist sweaters, inspired by Picasso and Braque.

As society broadened its traditional perimeters to include the bohemians of the creative world, so couture also enlarged its area of inspiration from past mode to modern art. This was not the old rue de la Paix couture, however, catering solely for a traditional tiny moneyed elite. The new patrons were as adventurous about their dress as they were about the books they wrote or read or the paintings they bought. They were looking for modern couture. In the face of such stiff competition, the old order gracefully withdrew from the fray – leaving the new young couturiers such as Patou and Chanel to reign unchallenged until October 1929.

Not only were there the completely new private clients (and many more of them), but the possibilities – as Patou quickly perceived – for wholesaling designs by selling models for reproduction in thousands to retailers from all over the world, now seemed to be limitless. More and more women were working, leading some kind of public life, earning money of their own. In every large city shops were opening to cater for them, and these shops needed the prestige and the inspiration of couture copies 'straight from Paris'. The couture industry which before the war had really been dressmaking for a small elite on a craft basis with occasional excursions into model reproduction now found itself on the verge of becoming a large-scale industry; Patou among others soon realized it needed a new approach, not only to design but also to promotion and marketing.

It took couture, led by Chanel and Patou, about five years
to change. Importantly, Patou invented what he always called
les riens, the little nothings like perfumes and accessories which
are the mainstay of the Paris fashion industry today.

Between 1919 and the mid-thirties couture became one of
France's major twentieth-century industries. Patou had much
to do with encouraging the twentieth-century idea of good
design for the mass market.

After the high waisted look of the prewar collections, the
waist gradually crept down, the line straightening out into
almost flat pannelling. First, in 1919, came the long-waisted
fantasy 'shepherdess' dresses with belled skirts from Patou
and a number of other couturiers. These, interestingly
enough, were worn all the way through the twenties by debu-
tantes, and Madame Lanvin built an enormous business
based on her versions of this look. By 1921, some skirts had
narrowed and the heavy, straight ankle-length skirt worked
in panels and often with further flying panels over the top,
hanging from the hip, had become fashionable. This created
a problem for a couture business still starved of fabrics, for
these flat, straight, long dresses needed detail – whether print,
jacquard or embroidery.

Just one decorative device was available, and therefore
rapidly seized upon by Patou and by Chanel for their first
prewar collections – naive Russian embroidery. There was a
sad reason for this. The many aristocratic
Russian émigrée women who had come to Paris
after the revolution were, by this time, begin-
ning to realize that their return to a Russia
with a restored monarchy might be indefinitely post-
poned and their money was running out. Many of them were
beginning to feel the pinch, and dressmaking and embroidery
learned in the past merely as an accomplishment became for
many Russian women a lifeline.

To help her fellow countrywomen, the Grand Duchess
Marie Pavlovna, a daughter of the Grand Duke Paul Alex-
androvitch and first cousin of the last Tsar, started a small
company which specialized in intricate, folkloric *russe* embroidery inspired by traditional peasant designs. As a means
of helping those princesses, grand duchesses and countesses
stranded in Paris, it was a very practical notion. The company

was called Kitmir (after the Grand Duchess's pet pekinese) and its two main customers in the years 1920 and 1921 were Patou and Chanel, both of whom produced 'Russian' collections of long-waisted dresses with floating panels of coloured embroidery, worn with embroidered boyar waistcoats. These clothes were still heavy and clumsy, but the needlework lent them a touch of vivid colour and fantasy.

The Russian peasant look was the first really new fashion trend since the war. It appears clumsy today, and, when one considers what Patou achieved in the way of artful simplicity in later collections, very cluttered. At the time, however, it was perceived as fresh and new, and the growing number of Patou clients loved it, for it represented luxury and fantasy, two qualities that had disappeared with the outbreak of war.

There have always been ethnic influences in women's clothes – the Turkish harem look, for example, that became so popular in France in the eighteenth century returned in the mid-nineteenth century and again in the late 1970s. Poiret's oriental revival was the first 'costume' look of fashion in the twentieth century, but the influence from the steppes, so evident in the 1921 collections, was unusual in that it was inspired by peasant motifs rather than aristocratic, starting a folkloric trend that fashion has followed, from time to time, to this day.

The Grand Duchess was not a clever businesswoman, but her embroideries were the only novelties then obtainable in France and, initially, her business was a tremendous success. Fashion followers read at that time of Patou's 'Hungarian vests with grey grounds on which are coloured embroideries. The embroideries on the shoulders and the sleeves are the good new details which will revive the suit,' said French *Vogue* of Patou's autumn 1919 collection, intended for spring 1920.

The Grand Duchess became a close friend and frequent companion of Patou's during the first half of the twenties and they often travelled together to such fashionable resorts as the Riviera, Patou's house in Biarritz and Deauville, particularly in the mid-twenties, after she had divorced her second husband. At one time it was rumoured that they might marry – certainly Elsa Maxwell mentions it in her memoirs.

Many reasons could be advanced as to why Patou never married. Perhaps, as already suggested, he was too involved in work to contemplate a permanent relationship with one woman. He was certainly promiscuous, for even in that free and easy day he was known for the many casual affairs he had with women who ranged from society hostesses to workers in his couture house. But of all his romances, the Grand Duchess was the only one who seemed to last any length of time. She settled in New York in the early thirties, however, where she designed dresses for Bergdorf Goodman and ran Russian charities.

Patou's vigorous and elaborate designs for these first collections up to 1921, coupled with the fact that he was beginning to attract personal publicity, were an instant success with his first clients. With these early collections, Patou established himself in the minds of smart women as a very 'French' designer. His sure way with line and cut, while still submerged in floating panels, drooping hemlines and embroideries, was beginning to emerge. But perhaps most important of all, he established himself as a couturier who really liked women, and wanted to make even the dumpiest client look feminine.

'It is Jean Patou the man, as much as Jean Patou the artist, who puts together his collections,' a fashion journalist later reported in 1924, and continued: 'He creates his collections not for women in general, but for the woman of his dreams, the woman he would like to see beside him in his salon or in a theatre or restaurant. He follows her through every stage of her day, and for this reason a woman can choose her whole wardrobe from him.' His clothes were always conceived for ease of movement, they always have an element of hurry and dash about them.

By the spring of 1922, Patou had begun to clarify his ideas, no doubt helped by his growing friendships with so many artists and designers of the art-deco period. Beige was, as *Vogue* reported, the favoured colour that spring; and Patou produced a particularly beautiful collection in which he employed the device of insetting geometric godets for the first time, to give a slim line which hid, in its clever cutting, enough fabric to make possible athletic dashing movement. These godets are ziggurat-shaped, presaging the skyscraper motifs that were to be so definitive a feature of later twenties design. A slim, ruler-straight broadcloth cape, for instance,

in a shade of beige tinted with green shown in *Vogue* in 1922, with jagged, angular inserts, giving a freedom of movement without bulk, exemplifies the Patou look.

For the mid-season collection in 1922, Patou adopted an even more severe line, prompting *Vogue* to describe his simple, rough, dark brown coat trimmed with Persian lamb as 'straight as string'.

Baron Gayne de Meyer was one of the leading photographers at this time. He had worked for *Vogue* for many years, but had been lured away to *Harper's Bazaar* by its proprietor, Randolph Hearst. He was often employed by Patou to take publicity photographs and the two men had a great deal in common. Both were extremely ambitious, and although the Baron was a notorious homosexual, he seemed to get on very well with Patou.

The Baron was an extraordinary man, who took photographs of such luminous delicacy that they have never been surpassed. Married to a woman whom most of society believed was Edward VII's natural child, the Baron and his Baroness were admitted to high society on two continents, so that his contacts were invaluable, first to Edna Woolman Chase at *Vogue*, and subsequently at *Harper's Bazaar* where he was allowed not just to photograph, but also to write articles and couture collection notes.

One day in 1923, the Baron asked Patou: 'Have I ever told you how much discussion the name of Jean Patou provokes?' And he continued, 'Some say you are one of the greatest artist-couturiers of the day, and others say you are merely a marvellous *organisateur*, but what,' the Baron asked, 'do you have to say about this?'

'An artist?' replied Patou. 'Does anyone really suppose I am an artist? I can't believe it. I don't consider myself to be an artist at all; there is absolutely no need of being one in order to be a successful couturier. What is needed is taste, a sense of harmony, and to avoid eccentricity.'

Patou told Baron de Meyer that he believed uncivilized people could have no taste, for taste was the result of many generations. 'Taste is intangible, elusive and yet all-important, a supreme and essential quality for successful dressmaking. But to be an artist – no, there is no need for that. Take the Russians . . . their artists have influenced our theatrical costumes considerably, especially in colour and embroideries, but I cannot,' said Patou, 'recall ever having heard of any great Russian couturier.'

De Meyer then asked Patou the question that had been debated in some of the drawing rooms of Paris. Did he actually create his own models, or was he a couture Svengali, leaching the talents of other, nameless designers? Patou was characteristically straightforward about this.

'I wouldn't know how to design,' he replied. 'I couldn't even if I wanted to, for I can't draw, and a pair of scissors in my hands becomes a dangerous weapon. Consequently, my organization must differ from most other dressmaking establishments and I have what I call my laboratory. Here designers are at work producing sketches both for new models and embroideries.'

Months before he started a collection, Patou gave his designers antique textiles, bits of embroideries, 'in fact precious documents to derive inspiration from, with special indications of styles and colourings I wish them to develop.'

The results were then submitted to Patou, modified, corrected and improved upon until they satisfied him; and only then did he pass them on to the *modellistes* with instructions as to their execution. 'Therefore all models are combined by me and no trials are made without my being present. Installed in an armchair, smoking, I watch and criticize the work until each model is perfect.'

Patou believed that this method of editing explained the apparent diversity of his collections which, nevertheless, imparted an impression of one distinct personality.

To produce a collection of three hundred models, Patou often had to make six hundred and then prune – a much more common method of working in the twenties than today. Most couturiers at that time cut and draped their designs on the models, working from swatches and from sketches produced in their design studios, or brought in from freelance fashion sketchers. It was virtually unknown for a leading couturier to sketch, and it was not until the rise of Christian Dior (who had started as a design assistant to Lucien Lelong) that designers sketched rather than draped on the figure. This concentration on the physical reality of a dress or coat design was undoubtedly a legacy from the dressmaker origins of the couture business.

Patou was the first of what might, in modern terms, be described as a design editor, as he had a very large design studio producing for him the raw materials of textile designs, historical costume references and detailed sketches from which he could then assemble his collection. The *croquis* or design drawings that now form one of the most important records of couture in the twenties were always drawn after the collection had been completed.

Textile design, in common with other applied arts, reached new levels of aesthetic and technical achievement in the twenties. The art-deco period has been called the last era of total style, and fashion textiles profited from this crossfertilization of art and fashion. Cubist lamés jostled with Vorticist jacquards and even plain fabrics were subtly woven to create new effects. Couturiers' designs were rated not just on their proportions and silhouettes, but on colour and on textile design. Through the twenties Patou experimented with blues and with tinted beiges of all shades – sometimes they would have a green cast, sometimes a pink.

Patou worked closely with such suppliers as the Lyons silk mill, Bianchini Ferier, which had Raoul Dufy under contract with them through the twenties. The huge textile company, Rodier, which made dress and furnishing fabrics, was another important supplier. Rodier were the original manufacturers of the knitted jersey Chanel did so much to popularize, but early in the twenties they launched a series of superb handwoven wool and cashmere clothes inspired by the French Colonial exhibits at the 1922 Marseilles exhibition.

These beautiful fabrics were inspired by decorative motifs from Annam (now part of Vietnam), Cambodia (now the Khmer Republic), Guinea in West Africa and Equatorial Africa, woven into fine white or off-white woollen grounds in such a way that when the dress was designed, the motifs could form a border, or an asymmetric effect on a bodice or on a sleeve. Brilliant colours set against natural white or ivory were an important influence in the twenties.

Patou eventually became so intimately involved with the creation of new colours and new types of fabric that Rodier

40

partly financed his expansion of the business in the mid-twenties.

During this period of fusion between art and fashion, Patou was profoundly influenced by a fellow Zouave officer, the painter Bernard Boutet de Monvel, who worked with Sue and Mare and with whom the couturier was intimately connected all through the twenties. Boutet de Monvel drew many of Patou's most beautiful advertisements, helped him decorate his apartment, his salon and, later, his summer house at Biarritz. Boutet de Monvel had been one of the group of artists commissioned by the publisher Lucien Vogel to contribute to the exquisite but shortlived fashion album *Gazette du Bon Temps*. The group, which included Georges Lepape, Benito and André Marty, had worked for Vogel contributing superb fashion illustrations of prewar couture. Each one was a fully conceived painting that told a story, and each was hand-tinted. *Gazette du Bon Temps* was probably the most beautiful fashion magazine ever produced, and influenced layouts and illustration in *Vogue, Harper's Bazaar* and *Fémina* throughout the twenties. Due to paper shortages, however, Lucien Vogel was forced to close it in 1915, and, by the end of the war, he was editing the French edition of American *Vogue*.

When Boutet de Monvel returned from the war, he joined the Compagnie des Arts Français. One of the two founders, the designer André Mare, had begun to practise interior decoration in 1910, and after working with the architect Louis Sue on the decorations to celebrate the end of the war in 1918, joined forces with Sue to found this company. They worked with a highly talented group of artists and craftsmen – Boutet de Monvel, Gustave-Louis Jaulmes, who specialized in tapestry design and mural paintings, Paul Vera, a painter and sculptor, and André Marty, whose fashion illustrations had an eighteenth-century delicacy and refinement much in demand at *Vogue* and *Fémina*.

Some of the most beautiful interiors this group created were for Patou. First, in 1921, when he had really begun to make his name and was beginning to make his fortune too, the group decorated the rue St Florentin. They were less concerned with creating startling, high-fashion interiors than following, albeit in a modern manner, traditional French values of elegance. They created furniture in highly polished wood, with soft, slightly bulbous outlines. Each piece was carved in bas-relief with stylized flowers, derived from eighteenth-century wood engravings. The company painted Patou's huge salons in a subtle, strange shade of ash beige, painting the chairs and their caned seats to match, and designed round natural blond wood tables. Sue and Mare retained the noble eighteenth-century proportions of the rooms, emphasizing them with huge faceted mirrors. Nothing has been changed.

The company's influence on Patou did not end with their designs for his salon. Patou was an innovator, probably one of the first couturiers, in common with Chanel (who had been prompted by Misia Sert), to realize that fashion benefits by being part of a coherent movement creating a crossfertilization of ideas from interior designs to clothes and accessories to technology and high art. For the rest of his life, Patou commissioned these leaders of art-deco design to create every perfume bottle, every piece of furniture in his couture house, to decorate his apartment in Paris and his house in Biarritz, where they created every aspect of the interior design including all the furniture, the curtains and carpets, and the light fittings. Everything was specially designed for Patou. And, later, they even designed his tomb.

Sue and Mare's preoccupation with a total look, carefully thought out and harmonized to the last detail, was echoed by Patou's design concepts in his collections: huge though they were, all were coherent, following a decisive line, making a single stylish statement. Perhaps the most perfect reflection of his involvement with the major decorative design movements of his time can be seen in the series of cubist sweaters he began designing in 1924. There had always been a geometric element in the way Patou had constructed his clothes. As early as 1921 the geometric inserts that were to become one of his trademarks had appeared in a black cape. But with the cubist sweater, he took inspiration directly from an art movement, and married it with the other great preoccupation of the time – sport. Cubism interpreted in sweaters suddenly became an international craze. Patou extended it to matching skirts, bags and, most successfully, to bathing costumes. Patou was equally influenced by Sue and Mare's more romantic, floral eighteenth-century approach to art-deco, the other side of the modernist coin, and he commissioned prints in this mood, featuring flat flowers on three-dimensional grounds.

Patou's instinct for showmanship and publicity of a rather exalted kind led him, once he had achieved his high standards of workmanship and presentation, to institute an event that in the successful years ahead was to become an important twice-yearly fixture in the Paris social calendar: the *répétition générale*, or full dress rehearsal, held immediately before the shows for clients and buyers. Before this, couture houses had simply shown their collections on opening day, following the excitement of the premiere, with all its attendant hysterics, with two shows a day for a month, and then the smaller shows for private clients.

Obviously, the first show was crucially important, for this was where the commercial buyers, those who would purchase models to copy for general distribution, chose their models. The American stores, by virtue of their spending power, traditionally had the first show to themselves. Next came the French shops, followed by the English shops such as Marshall & Snelgrove, and the English buyers such as Lady Victor Paget and Christabel Russell; and, finally, the Spanish and other representatives from all over the world, who translated these couture models into clothes for the comparatively wealthy, middle-class woman. The English buyers were mostly women who, finding their fortunes diminished as a result of the postwar slump, made a living by running hat shops or small dressmaking establishments for the English upper class. The most successful of them – Lady Victor Paget, Mrs Satterthwaite the tennis player, and Christabel Russell – relied on their social connections to provide them with a wealthy clientele for their copies of Parisian couture models.

Before Patou instituted the *répétition générale*, dress rehearsals, which took place the night before the premiere, were the province of the *vendeuses* and the workers, whose only opportunity this was to see the fruits of their labours in the attics. 'It is a study in contrast to see a wistful, spindle-legged twelve-year-old, clad in an ancient black frock and checked apron, devouring with her eyes the undulating mannequin in the golden creation from which it was the child's privilege to pull the basting threads,' commented one socially aware *Vogue* journalist at the time.

The credit for the invention of the *répétition générale* was claimed by Elsa Maxwell. This leviathan of the international café-society set had met Patou when she had been working for one of his rivals, Edward Molyneux. Molyneux and Patou were friendly rather than acrimonious competitors. When Elsa Maxwell first arrived in Paris, broke but with a reputation as a superb organizer, won by launching the Venice Lido as the place to see and be seen in the summer, Molyneux had quickly seized upon this unlikely looking asset. He realized that Elsa Maxwell might provide his entrée to an international clientele, with her many contacts with the international set. He asked her for some ideas on how he could achieve this and a *boîte de nuit* was her suggestion. What better way to meet potential clients than to be the owner of the smartest night club in Paris? Molyneux agreed and thus Miss Maxwell set out to create the night club to end all night clubs.

Le Jardin de ma Soeur, opened late in 1922, was an enchanted garden with a tiny dance floor and it stayed open late at night when everything else except the really low dives had closed. One went on there from a post-theatre supper at the Ritz (if one was conventional) or, if one was not, the Château Madrid or the Boeuf sur le Toit. It was an enormous social success, despite its great expense to Molyneux. The opening night came in a blaze of Maxwell-inspired publicity which reached tidal wave proportions with the news that her arch-enemy, the London hostess Emerald Cunard, had gatecrashed the party only to have her entrance sullied by one of the circling pigeons.

Molyneux (who had the intriguing habit, according to Elsa Maxwell, of bathing in red ink) lost money running the club, but he did gain the prestige and the notoriety that he needed to build his business. Later, when Patou was looking for someone to promote a suitable image and to ensure that his client list included not only the Parisians he had dressed with such confidence for the last six years but also the café society glitterati – who at that time were more likely to end up at Chanel – Molyneux suggested he hire Elsa Maxwell. Maxwell by the beginning of 1924 was at a loose end and in financial difficulties, since the police had forcibly closed Le Jardin de ma Soeur for infringements of the licensing laws.

Thus began a curious cooperation. The urbane, elegant Patou and the dumpy Miss Maxwell. Patou had already firmly established his reputation as an arbiter of modern taste. Elsa Maxwell, on the other hand, had established herself as a licensed buffoon, a jester and the doyenne of party-giving on two continents. For Molyneux, she created a night club, for Patou, she invented the gala couture opening.

In its combination of grandeur, socializing and hard-headed business, the *répétition générale* was very much in the style of its innovators, Patou and Elsa Maxwell. As a vehicle for publicity, Patou could not have bettered Miss Maxwell's luxurious solution. Invitations were restricted to a selection of the most important buyers, the most glamorous private clients (not necessarily those who spent the most money), and representatives of the most influential newspapers and maga-zines – all of whom were naturally flattered to be present, and thus well disposed to the show. Added to this rich mixture were diplomats and their wives and a sprinkling of the smart-est demimondaines dressed by Patou – famous *filles de joie* such as the Dolly Sisters. The result was a glittering social event with elegantly disguised commercial undertones.

Lillian Farley, who as the American model Dinarzade worked for Patou from 1924 to 1925, describes the *répétition générale* in her memoirs as it looked to her when she first modelled for Patou in the autumn of 1924.

The salons were brightly lighted with spotlights and flowers were everywhere. Tables, seating from two to six people, were placed in a single line around the walls, leaving space in the middle for the mannequins to show. On each table, in an ice-bucket, was either a bottle or a magnum of champagne. The names of the guests were on cards at each place.

As soon as everyone was seated, a footman presented an enormous mahogany box, containing a complete assortment of deluxe cigarettes and cigars.

A *maître d'hôtel* hastened to open the bottle on the table and the little assistant *vendeuses* in their beige uniforms passed round sample bottles of Amour Amour and Que Sais-Je, the new Patou perfumes.

Finally, everyone was ready, and the signal given to assemble for inspection in the last salon. Patou sat there with Madame Lucile, the *première*, Madame Louise, the *directrice*, and M. Georges, the *directeur* and they 'passed' every girl before she was allowed to show her costume.

Although Patou had seen every dress as it progressed from initial fabric clippings to the complete model, he had not yet been able to gauge the effect of the ensemble with the hat, which he had also designed, the shoes, always made for him by Greco, the handbag and the jewels loaned from Van Cleef & Arpels.

Often the final effect was better than anticipated, but sometimes 'Patou would shake his head . . . He would say, "No, I can't pass it, take it out . . . It is a very pretty dress, but it is not Patou." At least thirty models were cancelled.' He was enough of a showman to know that having made his name synonymous with a certain type of neat, tailored dress, he had to stick to it.

By 1924 Patou had established a distinctive look, evolved over the last three years from real sports clothes. Although the majority of his clients did not actually play tennis or golf, by 1924 the mood was such that they wanted to look as if they did, even if the most serious exercise they took was to walk into the Ritz for lunch. Patou had by now developed the language of pure sporting clothes into almost every area of women's dress, including full evening dress.

As Mrs Farley stepped through the doorway of the *cabine* to show her first dress, she had the impression, she remembers, of 'stepping into a perfumed, silk-lined jewel casket, so strongly charged was the atmosphere. The men in their correct black tailcoats with their sleek pomaded hair, the women in gorgeous evening dresses, plastered with jewels. It was so hot and the air was stifling with the mixed odours of perfumes and cigarettes.'

The sports and day clothes were shown first, another innovation that had been instigated by Patou when his collections became so big that splitting them in two became imperative. During the intermission, a buffet supper was served and then the evening dresses with their beautiful embroideries were shown. 'These were the big numbers in the collection,' explains Mrs Farley, 'to be photographed and sketched by every fashion periodical in the world and ordered as many as a hundred times by foreign buyers and clients.'

Patou had arrived.

3

Rosalind in Arden

By 1923 Patou had, with Chanel, Lanvin and the other major couturiers of the new order, established himself as a fashion leader. The stage was now set for the greatest period of Patou's success which would be based on his brilliant designs inspired by sportswear for the active woman. This golden era was ushered in suddenly and dramatically in the person of a brilliant, ungainly, temperamental tennis player: Suzanne Lenglen.

When she bounded on to the court at Wimbledon in 1921 wearing a white silk pleated skirt which only reached her knees, a straight white sleeveless cardigan and a vivid orange headband, smart women everywhere gasped. She was the personification of what they now knew they wanted to look like. The new woman had found her model, and she was, from head to toe, dressed by Jean Patou. She was revolutionary in her severe simplicity of dress – and in the details too. It looked as if Patou had taken the conventional man's cardigan and ripped the sleeves out for ease of movement. The new ideal embodied by Lenglen was to dominate the rest of the twenties and this athletic androgynous new type became known as *la garçonne*.

Une Garçonne was a novel by Victor Marguerite, published in 1922. It was risqué and very popular, concerning a Sorbonne student, Monique Lerbier, who cuts her hair, wears a man's jacket and tie, has a child out of wedlock, joins in orgies and toys with lesbianism. *Une Garçonne* became a runaway success, as French women en masse, closely followed by stylish women all over the world, set out to imitate Monique's style, and of course they wanted liberated, *sportif*, slightly androgynous clothes to match. Jean Patou, with his pleats,

Jean Patou and his sister
Madeleine photographed
with their grandfather
when Patou was about
twelve and his sister seven.
Patou

The tannery can be seen
behind the family's typical
mid-nineteenth-century
French bourgeois house.
This picture must have
been taken around the turn
of the century. *Patou*

Madeleine Patou (above) in a serge walking outfit, *circa* 1913. Her enchantingly neat 'French' looks were to be a continuing inspiration to her brother. *Patou*

Ten years later, Madeleine Patou had lost none of her elegance (top right), even when photographed in this eye-concealing straw hat. *Patou*

Captain Patou of the Zouaves (far right), bivouacked somewhere in Turkey — a far cry from the banquettes of Maxime's. *Patou*

Number 7 rue St Florentin at the time Patou took it over in 1914. In what must have been the Comtesse de Flahaut's bedroom, there is a cartouche containing the motif 'L'Amour c'est le roi'. Patou adapted this for his writing paper, changing the motto to 'La Mode c'est la reine'. Even today the secret passage connecting 7 rue St Florentin with the Hôtel Talleyrand still exists as a reminder of this great house's romantic past. *Patou*

Suzanne Lenglen, a star on and off the tennis court, and main instigator of the sportif mode, at Wimbledon in 1921. *Patou*

At the wheel of one of the first of many sports cars, Patou wears the obligatory aviator helmet. The car was a Farman, made by the aeroplane manufacturers. Later Patou was to change to Hispano Suizas. There are purchase records in Hispano Suiza's order books all through the twenties, and one, a sports model with a wooden body, owned by Patou can be seen in the Melbourne Museum. *Patou*

Suzanne Lenglen (far left) off court, wearing a Patou sweater and pleated skirt. *Patou*

Helen Wills (left), another tennis star dressed by Patou. *Patou*

Like many of his sportswomen clients, Helen Wills wore Patou clothes off court as well as on, as this photograph by Baron de Meyer shows (above). *De Meyer/Patou*

The sublime elegance of Louise Brooks, in a figured bronze lamé dress and jacket trimmed with fox fur. This dress was created for her when she was making *Lulu* with the German film director G. W. Pabst. *Patou*

Constance Bennett (top), the
American film star and close
friend of Louise Brooks, was
also a Patou client. *Patou*

Patou wears his own JP
monogrammed shirt (above) in a
photograph taken at the end of
the twenties. *Patou*

Patou at Longchamps (left)
in the late twenties. *Patou*

Patou's apartment in the rue de la Faisanderie (above) was designed for him by Sue et Mare. This is a corner of the top-floor studio, in whose sombre brown environs Patou did much of his work

The English actress Juliette Compton (top left) in a precursor of the new look. Late 1928. *Patou*

The actress Alys Delysia (left) was known for her exquisite taste in dress. Here she is photographed in Patou's silver lace dress, as simple as a bathing suit in its cut. *Mme Albin Grillot/Patou* his modern outlook, his sharp observation of the mood, was there to provide them.

'The keynote of the character of Jean Patou is modernity,' gushed the *Journal des Modes et Manners* in 1924.

Chez Patou one finds one of the few elevators in Paris which always runs, and one must live in Paris to appreciate the tremendous significance of this statement. Spacious salons, perfectly equipped design and dressmaking rooms, and a studio, its miniature stage lighted by the most improved methods for photography, are also included in the facilities of this astonishing institution.

It had taken Patou five years, but by 1924, at the age of forty-four, he had become a leading couturier. Patou never underestimated the intelligence of his clients. He did not believe in fashion diktats, as did Chanel, who was inclined to be emphatic in her pronouncements. Chanel told her clients that real jewellery was passé. That beige was best, that less was more. She used fashion as a medium through which she could comment on her times, and wanted her clients to follow her absolutely. Patou, on the other hand, felt that 'fashion should always reflect a woman's mind, it can never dictate to her,' as he told a journalist at the time. He designed clothes that required the personality of the individual, whims and caprices included, to work completely. There is always one element missing in a Patou design when it is hanging rather than being worn: the personality of the wearer. Patou turned clients out in style. It was undoubtedly Patou's style, but by some curious process the clothes always looked as if they had been the individual's own invention.

By 1923 Patou began to crystallize the 'look' for the new woman that would make him such a success for the rest of the twenties. But who was this woman? What did she want to look like? Who had made her clothes before? The answers were to be found in the appearance of the *nouveaux riches*. The wives of war profiteers who had suddenly found themselves with unlimited money, were ready to spend on high living, and sumptuous entertaining; and of course they wanted to dress magnificently, although they were, as yet, unsure of their taste.

These women regarded magnificent dresses, jewels, houses,

furniture and furs as the rightful trophies of peace. They were not able to afford such luxuries earlier, but now that they could their attitudes contrasted strongly with the pampered ladies of the Faubourgs. They considered themselves far too modern for the languid life of the boudoir and the salon; some had nursed in hospitals, driven ambulances, done war work of various kinds, or run their husbands' businesses in their absence at the front, and with all this had acquired a determination and independence too strong, too heady, to be extinguished by the niceties of old manners and morals. And those not engaged with war work had become similarly suffused with this new spirit.

Suzanne Lenglen summed up the essence of athletic youth, competitiveness and vigour. Her plain light colours and practical clothes transmitted this subconscious idea perfectly, and her sports clothes were to influence every facet of fashion design for nearly a decade.

Real bodies – sinews, muscles and all – rather than padded, distorted outlines, became important. These light fluttery clothes concealed little, and parallel with the development of the boyish, athletic type came a cult of physical fitness. Like the skyscrapers, the aerodynamics of the new cars, women's bodies became streamlined, spare and modern. Some women had no problems, many others found it difficult to change from an hourglass shape into a tube. Maisie, the enchanting heroine of Angus Wilson's pastiche *For Whom the Cloche Tolls*, was not alone in her rigorous dieting and the adoption of bust bindings. Rigorous dieting became common and many new reducing aids appeared. Gone were those 'meals, those endless meals', as Victoria Sackville-West described the Edwardian dinner parties of her youth. Physical fitness meant sport and eugenic dancing and many a twenties girl was to be seen emulating Isadora Duncan in a Greek tunic, exercising her newly slim body.

For some women, it was too late, and they were condemned to be hopelessly *démodé*. Flatness and sunburnt skin were the thing. No one really knows who started the craze for a suntan, but certainly it was stimulated by the new practice of going to the Riviera in the summer, rather than in the winter. Considering the care fashionable women had always taken to stay white even under the hottest sun to emphasize their

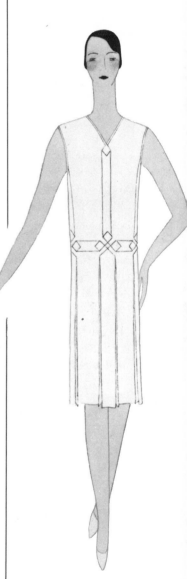

leisured status, it is surprising that a suntan became so popular so quickly. Chanel always claimed to have initiated this new look, but in reality she was only one enthusiast of many both in Europe and America.

A bronzed skin was part of the tremendous move toward a healthy body that continued throughout the twenties, culminating in the sinister youth movements of Hitler's Germany in the thirties. Americans were perhaps the most enthusiastic – Gerald and Sarah Murphy at Cap d'Antibes, self-consciously stylish in matelot sweaters and suntans – but even such an established member of the *ancien régime* as the Duke of Windsor was photographed at Biarritz, or on board the yacht *Nahlin*, brown as a berry and wearing little-boy shorts, no shirt and espadrilles.

One remarkable result of this new look was the suddenness with which some lucky women assumed this new streamlined form. Voluptuous women such as the leader of Parisian avant-garde society, Misia Sert, for example, had been painted by Renoir as a glowing, rounded figure in a pink ballgown only ten years before, and yet now she looked more like a woman painted by Van Dongen, all angles and planes.

A new erogenous zone appeared to replace ample busts and smooth creamy shoulders: legs became visible for the first time since Madame Récamier's had been glimpsed through the transparent muslins of her *Directoire* gown in the early 1800s. As the new focal point, legs had to be straight and slim and many were the ankle exercises done in the name of fashion. In winter, stockings had to be of the finest silk, rolled up to garters. In summer, the ideal was deeply sunburnt bare legs. Smooth and very, very thin.

The Spanish Duchess de Penaranda got the look absolutely right, according to Cecil Beaton. A deeply bronzed skin offset by a skimpy white pleated dress, enormous pearls matching her white teeth, black hair brilliantined back into a dark, glossy cap, and six-inch spiked shoes with ankle straps added up to the look.

Suzanne Lenglen was the real personification of the new look, however. Through Raymond Barbas, Patou and Lenglen became firm friends: he always made her clothes and she in turn became the first sports star, in 1921, to endorse a designer's work. As a living advertisement of Patou's look,

51

she may have helped him to define it, for she had her own point of view about clothes both on and off the tennis court. In recognizing the value of this sort of approval, by someone universally admired and respected rather than by elegantly idle society ladies, Patou showed how far ahead of his time he was.

Lenglen was in many ways an unlikely model, having rather masculine features, but she brought something to wearing clothes – and to tennis – that was totally new. She possessed an arresting personality and an unrivalled grace which is still remembered by those who saw her play in the twenties. Although her face was not beautiful, with its beaky nose and firm chin, she possessed a dynamic elegance, like many women with imperfect features but outstanding personal style.

'For playing a man's type of game, she needed freedom of movement. Off came the suspender belt, and she supported her stockings by means of garters above the knee. Off came the petticoat and she wore only a pleated skirt; off came the long sleeves and she wore a neat, short-sleeved vest.' What Lord Aberdare did not emphasize in his book, *The Story of Tennis*, was that the short-sleeved vest was itself a revolutionary garment, never before seen in such a context, or indeed in such a fabric, being derived from a man's woven cloth waistcoat. Patou had designed a genuinely revolutionary garment, which was not missed by those who watched Suzanne Lenglen at the time. Her appearance at Wimbledon in 1922 caused much comment, and each new fashion of dress which she introduced was widely copied.

The smart set from 1920 passed their summers bronzing themselves on the Riviera rather than lounging pallidly indoors. They played golf all year round, skied in St Moritz during the winter, and sailed at Newport in the early summer. And if they were not *sportif*, they followed those who were, and dressed as if a mashie niblick was to hand. Fashionable society had been hailed by the wild, and it wanted to dress accordingly. Even when they were indoors, in cocktail bars, smart restaurants, or in night clubs like Le Jardin de ma Soeur, they still wanted to give the impression of outdoor energy and healthy youth. As Cecil Beaton put it, 'Lillian Russell and the Gibson girls had turned into Rosalind in the Forest of Arden.'

Skirts continued their slow ascent, first apparent before the First World War. Hair was shingled from the war years and then Eton-cropped, until by the late twenties the accepted look had become as standard as a school uniform and about as feminine. Girls had become good chaps, and there was scarcely any difference between the dress for a child of eight or a woman of eighteen, thirty or sixty.

Patou dressed them, more successfully than anyone else, these direct, brown, thin girls with short lacquered or sun-bleached hair and an active bouncy walk. His clean, simple clothes had banished all extraneous fripperies and they were as right in their milieu as the skyscraper was right for New York. It took Patou four collections from 1922 to perfect it, but by the autumn of 1924 the change was total, thought out to the last pleat.

Patou's attitude to this new boyish woman surely contrasted strangely with his own flagrantly heterosexual taste: it would not have been surprising if he had promoted elaborate, rather sexist design, emphasizing a fragile femininity, celebrating the natural curves, rather than advocating the planed and angled *garçonne*. Pehaps it was simply because Patou was not deeply involved with one woman that he was able to view women objectively, yet with a sympathy that enabled him, with an obvious sensitivity, to create clothes that combined the new spirit of freedom and yet appealed to men.

Patou's external image of his private life – his recklessness, his 'little amours', the general air he assumed as if he were in an eighteenth-century play – was really a mask he wore, more as a publicity device, in order to further his real ambition which seems simply to observe and dress women who were intelligent, lively and modern, in clothes which matched their aspirations, without neutering them, and with none of the lesbian undertones of Chanel. He raced cars, shot, fished, played tennis, sailed, raced his speedboat and wore correct sporting clothes for all these activities. Since in his own dress he favoured the *Anglais* look, he was aware that even formal men's clothes had, for the last century, been influenced by Beau Brummell and by traditional English sporting clothes, all perfectly designed for their function.

The transition to designing clothes created by women's wish to participate in sports cannot have been difficult for Patou, as he was already familiar with the design language. The first occasion on which these 'sports' clothes made an appearance in his salons was in his summer 1922 collection. His skirts, in common with the rest of Paris, were still long, at about three inches above the ankle, but the line was slimmer, much more supple and generally lighter in effect. 'This Patou frock of white kasha would be most convenient for sportswear,' wrote *Vogue* in June. 'It has fan-shaped pleated panels on the skirt and one's monogram on the blouse. A widely belted coat of red and black blazer-striped toile is worn with it.'

This is the first time the Patou monogram appeared. It spawned many imitators at the time, including the Chanel interlocking Cs and the Hermès H, and indeed it was an innovation which many designers have used since. Women had earlier had their initials embroidered on their underwear or their handkerchiefs, but they had never before flaunted the designer's identity. It took Patou's shrewdness to realize that these new and newly wealthy customers needed the prestige of a visible label. Imitators of the visible label still flourish today with Gloria Vanderbilt jeans, for example, the permanent appeal of the famous Gucci G, and CD, unmistakably Dior.

In July 1923, *Vogue* wrote of another of Patou's designs, 'Patou is responsible for the success of a sports jacket made of a watermelon red cotton fabric embroidered in white cotton thread to give a quilted effect. Black gaufre [finely pleated] crêpe trims it. The pleated skirt is of white crêpe-de-chine.' The skirt was still very long at just a few inches above the ankle, and it was to take Patou another year to bring his skirts up to the knee, where they stayed for some years.

By the end of 1923, Patou had further crystallized his sporty, neat line. The striped blazer toiles Patou was then using were directly stolen from the masculine sporting wardrobe, and were in fact inspired by English I Zingari cricketing coats, and Leander rowing blazers.

'My clothes are made to practise *le sport*,' Patou explained to a journalist writing for an American syndication service, NEA, in 1924. 'No sportsman or sportswoman will find in them the slightest mistake. I have aimed at making them pleasant to the eye and allowing absolute liberty of movement.' Sportswomen such as the aviatrix Ruth Elder commissioned entire sporting wardrobes from Patou at this time.

See that cardigan jacket belted at the hips so that it does not fly up with the arm? That is how Mademoiselle Lenglen is dressing this year. Just a pleated skirt, quite short, of white crêpe-de-chine or marocain with a belted cardigan to match. You will notice that I combine the opposites. For instance, I have conceded to the return of more feminine fashions while introducing touches that are decidedly more masculine. Kasha jumper suits have high necks or still little collars with bows. That is piquant and pleasing. Every day one notices the influence of sport upon clothes. The sweater takes first place for morning and afternoon wear, and it is actually invading the evening mode.

To prove his point, Patou showed the NEA journalist some exquisite gowns which she describes as being nothing more than embroidered low-necked sweaters, worn over skirts. For walking, he explained that he considered coats and skirts

were best. These he made in English materials he called 'beautiful and mannish'. Most of them were specially designed for him by Linton Tweeds in Scotland, but nearly all were in very English pastel colours. The journalist concluded that to 'look smart was merely the cheapest attribute of the boulevards. To feel and look at home in your clothes; to aim for quietness, correctness and distinction – surely this is ideal.'

In 1924, a new sort of heroine took the world literally by storm. The Armenian novelist friend of Nancy Cunard and bon viveur, Michael Arlen, published his best-selling novel *The Green Hat*. Its heroine, Iris Storm, would have come straight out of a Patou collection.

She was tall, not very tall, but as tall as becomes a woman. Her hair, in the shadow of her hat, may have been any colour, but I dared swear that there was a tawny whisper to it . . . she stood carelessly like the women in Georges Barbier's almanacks, *Falbalas et Franfreluches*, who know how to stand carelessly. Her hands were thrust into the pockets of a light brown leather jacket – pour le sport – which shone quite definitely in the lamplight: it was wide open at the throat and had a high collar of some fur of a few minks. One small red elephant marched across what I could see of her dress, which was dark and not pour le sport.

Iris Storm's green cloche hat and the Hispano Suiza became the rage.

It was in 1925, however, that Patou's sports designs really came into their own, and Patou acknowledged the growing importance of this part of his business when, on the advice of his brother-in-law, he opened a shop called Coin des Sports in January. It was a series of rooms on the ground floor of the rue St Florentin. Transformed, they were arranged separately to provide appropriate backgrounds for sports costumes. As a concept, the entire shop was modern, and it predated the boutique explosion of the sixties by forty years. Other couturiers, notably Lanvin, later followed suit.

One room was panelled with Scottish pitch pine and furnished with a huge fireplace in order to provide the proper canvas for the Harris tweeds that would find themselves just as at home on a Scottish moor. Another room contained a life-sized model of a racehorse made of shining brown leather (an idea Patou may well have picked up from an English

BERNARD
B. DE MONVEL

hunting tailor). A mannequin was perched on its back clad 'thoughtfully in a habit of brown suiting only a shade lighter than her mount'. Another room contained not only clothes for the smart fisherwoman, but the correct tackle too. With customary commercial acumen, Patou put the whole department in charge of an elegant and well-connected woman, Phillis, Vicomtesse de Janzé.

'Herself a typical English sportswoman, the aim and object of her direction will be to provide absolutely the right thing for the right place,' *Harper's Bazaar* explained in August 1925.

Are you going to the Lido in August? She will design you a bathing suit in which you will feel like a round peg in a round hole; for she has lounged on its hot sands herself at the proper moment, with the proper people and can equip you to do likewise . . . Are you meaning to play golf at Le Touquet? Madame de Janzé plays golf herself on all the links in Europe and knows just how to contrive those hidden pleats which will give you room for an efficient swing. Are you going to hunt in England? She hunts regularly from Melton, in the heart of Leicestershire.

One of a generation of aristocratic Englishwomen notable for their individuality and brilliance, a group that included Iris Tree, Nancy Cunard and Lady Diana Cooper, Phillis Boyd had stood out as wilder and more original than most. The granddaughter of King William IV and his beautiful and accomplished mistress, the actress Mrs Jordan, the mother of ten children by the King, Phillis Boyd was fascinating. She had shared a studio in Fitzroy Street during the First World War with Iris Tree and Nancy Cunard and all three of them led the lives of moneyed bohemians.

Phillis had studied at the Slade and had acquired a notoriety in London by wearing clothes similar to the biblical creations worn by Dorelia John. At the beginning of the twenties, however, she married a French sporting aristocrat, the Vicomte de Janzé, and abandoned Fitzroy Street in favour of the de Janzé chateau in Normandy, and when that palled, the racier society of Paris. She had unerring, if individual, taste and Cecil Beaton, always a great admirer, said of her that she had been the first woman ever to wear a short skirt. But it is not merely for being the first to raise her hems that Phillis de Janzé's name is remembered.

According to Beaton,

She was in many ways a remarkable personality. She had inherited artistic ability, charm and distinction, together with a beauty that was haunting and mysterious. She had the face of a puma, an extraordinary lithe line to her strong column-like neck and the fastidious walk of a crane.

It was extraordinary that England could produce something so essentially exotic as this Slavic-looking creature. With her pale complexion, knobby features, nose of a pugilistic cherub, full cherry lips and huge pale aquamarine eyes, rimmed with a sharp line of black as though from a fine mapping pen, dipped in Indian ink, it was little wonder that Lady de Grey would sail up to her and say, 'You are like Nijinsky.' Phillis's reply was typically surprising. 'I am, ain't I,' she laughed.

Her language was almost Restoration in its coarseness and frequently shocked contemporaries such as Diana Cooper, who nevertheless adored her. Her individuality, grace and elegance were undeniable. Balzac was a great passion of hers and she used to lie in bed, all day sometimes, unravelling a complicated Balzacian plot with all the determination and relish of someone untangling a much loved filigree chain. To see Phillis de Janzé turn her head, laugh, and swing her earrings from side to side was to 'marvel at a complete work of art. Phillis de Janzé and the twenties made a unique combination,' said Beaton. As soon as she arrived in Paris, she immediately exchanged her arts-and-crafts-inspired flowing peasant skirts and striped kerchiefs for neat little clothes from Patou.

She began to be described in the press and in magazines such as *Vogue* and *Fémina* as the best-dressed woman in France, and gave to the straight, short skirts and long-waisted jumper blouses, which were the hallmark of Patou's designs at that time, an extra chic and a personal flavour. She teamed these brisk sports clothes with impossibly high-heeled shoes of red leather, with straps round her ankles that must have looked like barbaric bracelets.

To Patou, Phillis de Janzé was the perfect model, the perfect counterpoint. Together they symbolized much that was fresh, modern and iconoclastic, infusing the heady atmosphere this collaboration created with their personal styles.

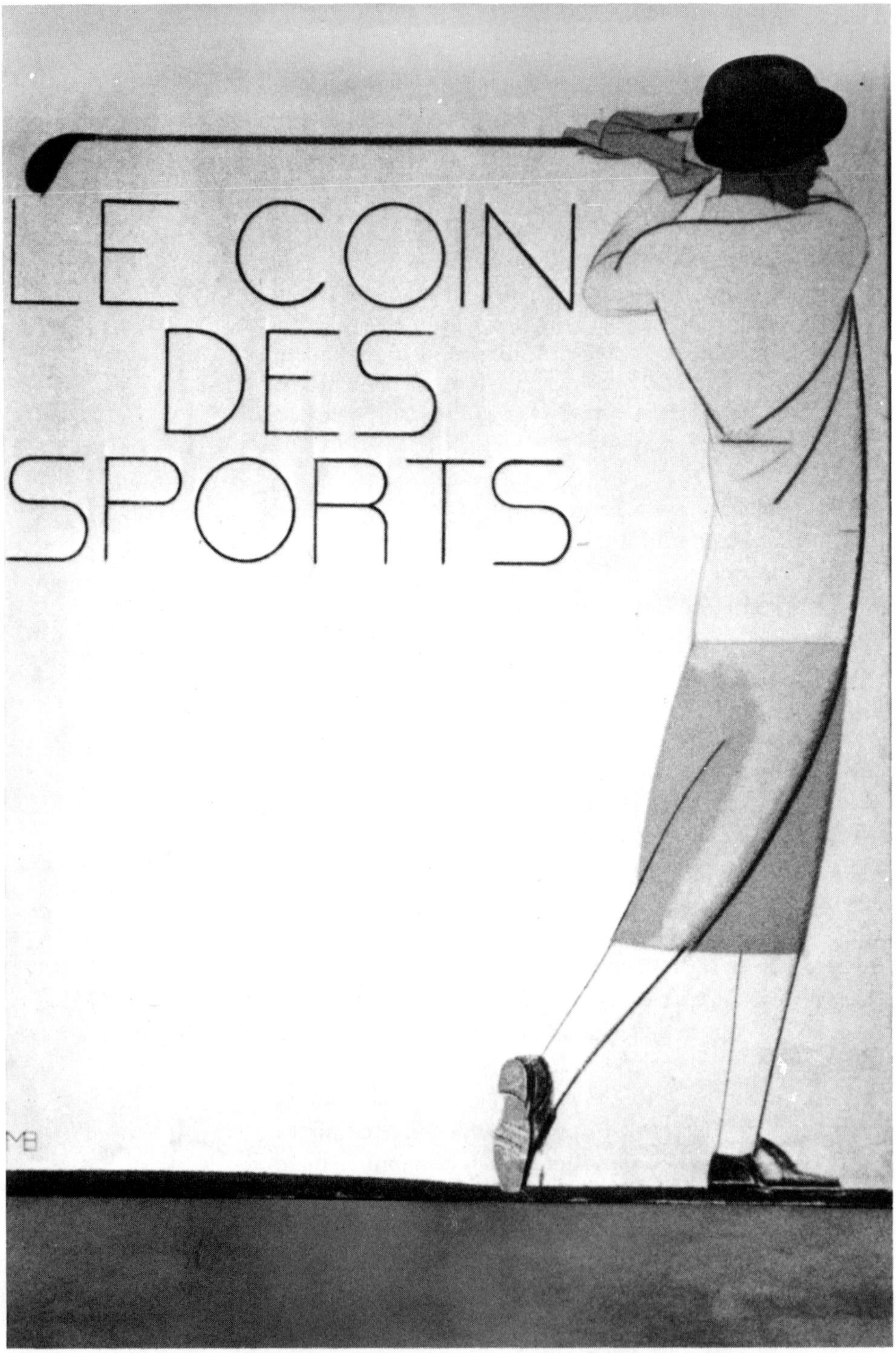
LE COIN
DES
SPORTS
MB

He worked very closely with Phillis de Janzé over every aspect of sports design, and they both insisted that the *sportif* clothes they sold should actually work, and not merely look fit for the golf course. However, it must be acknowledged that Patou did hedge his bets a little here and there. Raymond Barbas remembers a trip to St Moritz to promote some ski clothes in the late twenties 'that could not possibly have left the Palace Bar'. Patou then designed 'real' sports clothes, and also 'fashion' sports clothes for the woman who wanted to look sporty but whose only exercise was getting in and out of her Hispano Suiza.

'It is evident that there are today two distinct types in the dressmakers' clientele. The Latin type with its "outspoken" outlines and the Anglo-Saxon one which reaches its perfection in the long slender lines of the American silhouette,' said Patou in 1924.

The famous Patou bathing suits are a case in point. There were two sorts, those for serious swimmers and other models made for the sleepy afternoon hours under the Deauville tents or on the chaises longues of the lido beach. Those made for getting wet were carefully devised. When Patou asked his usual fabric suppliers for fabrics to make up these one-piece costumes, he discovered that no smart and beautiful fabric could be submerged in salt water without fading or shrinking. So he asked his weavers in the north of France to create some materials suitable for bathing which would both be chic and withstand a prolonged exposure to salt water.

In insisting on the practical qualities of swimming clothes, as well as an aesthetic value, Patou was well ahead of his time, and well justified the compliment paid by an American journalist in 1925 when she described him as the French couturier with an American mind. It was in the sixties, nearly thirty years after Patou's death, that the word 'ergonomic' was first used in a fashion context, meaning clothes designed for a specific purpose. Had Patou lived longer, he would no doubt have immediately understood the philosophy and popularity of jeans.

The same concern for practical detail was brought to all aspects of Patou's sportswear. Madame de Janzé consulted exponents of each sport for which the clothes were being designed, to find out first the requirements of bodily movement and then to reconcile them with the waistless, fluttering *garçonne* style. The tennis models, for instance, were shown to Suzanne Lenglen, who imparted very precise information to Patou, for she was used to having her sports clothes made from her own ideas. And so the Patou tennis frock was created. The Coin des Sports was an immediate success with Patou's clients and attracted a large proportion of the international country-club set that was to be found playing bridge indoors and almost every conceivable sport outdoors.

The sports influence continued, as far as Patou was concerned, until he completely altered the silhouette and dropped hemlines at the end of the twenties. But, in a sense, this way of designing is more relevant today than ever before, bearing out the maxim Patou understood so well that 'the sports wear of one generation is the formal wear of the next.'

Patou-sur-Mer

By the middle years of the 1920s, Jean Patou had not only established himself beside the other Parisian top-line couturiers but had made a name for himself with his sports and swimwear designs – and indeed with his original philosophy of couture, underlined by his continuing rivalry with Chanel. The move to the golf course and to the beaches, in particular, did not happen overnight. At the beginning of the twenties the French Riviera was still the province of the moneyed middle-aged who wintered there. The new rich took about five years to discover the delights of the Alpes Maritimes, and the international drinking season, as the Côte d'Azur summer came to be called, was really launched single-handedly by Elsa Maxwell, who was hired by the Société des Bains de Mer to 'do something' about Monte Carlo. She it was who persuaded café society that the Riviera had much to offer in the summer, using the same methods that had been such a success in her popularization of the Venice Lido.

The secret of Elsa Maxwell's success was quite simply a talent to amuse. To the moneyed international café society she acted as a Butlin's redcoat of fun, exhorting them to dress up as babies, planning masked balls or come-as-someone-you-hate parties. She entertained them royally, always spurred on by a private wish to break into the international set, or by concerns with vested interests such as the Société des Bains de Mer, or the hoteliers along the Lido. And where Miss Maxwell went for profit, her international society friends followed. And why not? She was amusing, had deliciously daring ideas and she was always fun.

Her other secret was the best address book in the world. Private telephone numbers of such international luminaries as the Duke and Duchess of Windsor, Lady Mendl – people who would attract the rest of the set to wherever they were at the time. She was the first of the big-time modern public-relations ladies, perhaps the inventor of the business. Elsa Maxwell was best, ultimately, at publicizing herself, and therefore landing these extraordinary commissions. There has never been anyone like her for creating high life and setting new trends.

As late as 1926, however, the American expatriate friend of Scott Fitzgerald's, the elegant Gerald Murphy, was considered eccentric in choosing to live in the South of France in the summer. He spent much of his time clearing seaweed off a deserted beach at Cap d'Antibes, which until his arrival had been the province of the local fisherman.

Deauville had been popular before the First World War, but only for early summer weekends, peopled by a mixture of the old Faubourg society and the demimonde, among them Coco Chanel. Although drawn by the lure of polo and gambling, this rather racy society would not have entertained the notion of spending a whole summer there. However, the introduction of the motorcar and the windswept tourer helped to change this. Of more fundamental influence was the fact that the new rich needed something to do in the summer – and they had neither country houses nor friends who did. Neither did the majority of foreigners who visited France, or who made their home there in the twenties. Café society, linked as it was by newly acquired wealth, rather than by inherited money, was drawn to resorts where they could amuse themselves with others of their kind. And so summer resorts, catering to the tastes of the exotic, gradually became established.

In 1924, Patou opened a shop for bathing and sportsdresses in Deauville, reassuring his clients that 'if need be, a modern woman may wear a sporting-looking ensemble both in the morning and for lunch.' He reasoned that his clientele should never be too far from a Patou maison, and if they were going to spend spring and summer weekends in Deauville, then they would need to have somewhere to spend their money. A Patou shop would help them fill those idle moments between watching polo matches and tea dances.

To a keen observer such as Patou, the migration to sunnier

climes meant that in the latter half of the twenties he, as did his clients, spent nearly half the year in one or other resort such as Deauville or Biarritz. Deauville was, of course, the most convenient. The old guard as well as most of the new now went there for spring and summer weekends, and the fact that the fashionable set of Deauville survived the watershed of the war was due largely to the efforts of its popular socialite mayor, Henri Letellier, often caricatured in the daily press such as *Le Matin* by the artist Sem, who made his summer headquarters there.

Letellier had become mayor before the war, and held the position through the twenties. He was, even for that gregarious era, an extraordinarily social man, independently wealthy, and publisher of the gossip sheet *Paris Journal*. Throughout the twenties, he staged a tireless round of events during the season to amuse his capricious patrons and ensure their allegiance to the town: events such as polo – the most popular spectator sport; Rose Queen contests – they were crowned ad infinitum; *thé dansants* – held every day in one or other of the big hotels, so that smart women could show off their new clothes; gambling – ever popular; and endless bathing-beauty contests of a kind rather more refined than the modern equivalent. Nice girls showed off their new *pour la plage* outfits, rather than large areas of their anatomy. These bathing-beauty contests were in fact outdoor fashion shows.

As his aide-de-camp during much of the twenties, Letellier had enlisted the services of Erskine Gwynn, who was a distant cousin of the Vanderbilt family and typical of many young, rich expatriate Americans on the Paris scene. He knew almost everyone. His continuous, if disturbing, presence in Deauville (he had the habit of getting into fights, which saw him in court more than once) ensured Letellier of the lavish patronage of the Long Island country-club set. Vanderbilts, Rockefellers, Fishs, Stotesburys all sent their sons to Paris to play. They could afford to live very comfortably and practise the art of the boulevardier, secure with trusts and bonds, as well as stocks and shares.

Scions of the American aristocracy such as Harry Crosby, nephew of the financier, J. P. Morgan, or Lucius Beebe, wit,

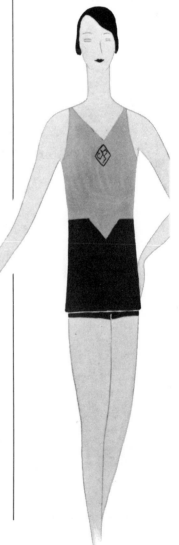

dandy and chronicler of the very rich in the *New York Post* and later in books – whose uncle Ned Center had lived in Paris since the nineties – felt most at ease not in Back Bay Boston, or New York's Fifth Avenue, but at the Ritz bar in Paris.

These wealthy sons of stockbrokers, Harvard and Princeton dilettants, loved to read of such typical Gwynn exploits as being shanghaied by his friends and sent home to America on the *Mauretania*, possessing only the clothes he stood up in, which happened to be an old suit of golfing clothes. Gwynn's presence in Deauville ensured its place on the circuit.

The other attraction of Deauville was the opportunity it afforded to watch women. Patou loved the place for this reason, as well as for the gambling and sport. But, as always, he was sufficiently sagacious to mix business with pleasure. He opened a shop in what was really an enlarged beach hut on the boardwalk, and it was an immediate success. Although his customers bought their formal clothes such as suits, dresses, evening dresses and furs in Paris, where the necessary fittings could be arranged, sports clothes were less demanding. The cubist sweaters, the bathing suits or an amusing scarf could be bought at Deauville on impulse, off the peg, or with only minor alterations.

Patou was becoming ever more preoccupied with sports clothes. Designs for Suzanne Lenglen had been followed by well-publicized wardrobes created specially for Helen Wills Moody and Mlle Vlasty, other tennis players of the first rank. Strong, striking women such as these presented the sort of challenge Patou relished, and the aviatrix Ruth Elder's wardrobe, which went right through from sportswear to evening dress, had attracted high praise in the press, always nectar to Patou. 'I found her very feminine,' he said, 'a woman who could carry an evening gown with as much grace as she did her flying clothes. She gave us the idea that I would have to begin creating aviation clothes for feminine fliers.'

Scott Fitzgerald summarized the mood, describing Jordan Baker in *The Great Gatsby* as wearing her 'evening dress, all her dresses, like sports clothes – there was a jauntiness about her movements as if she had first learned to walk upon golf courses on clean crisp mornings.' Even Ernest Hemingway was not unaware of the implications of this way of dressing.

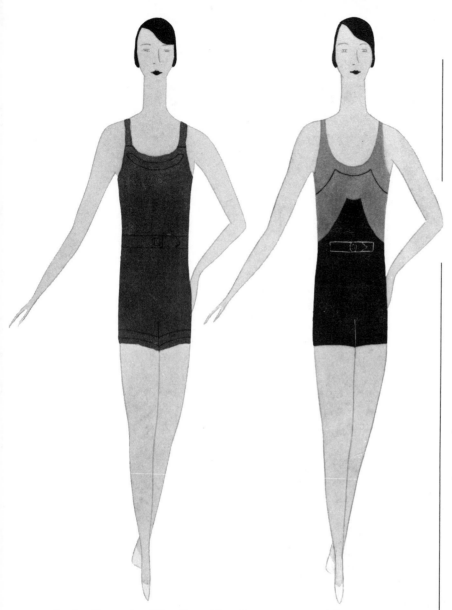

Lady Brett in *The Sun Also Rises* wore a 'slip-over jersey
sweater and a tweed skirt and her hair brushed back like a
boy's. She started all that.'

Patou applied the sinewy language of these sporting clothes
to everything he designed from 1924 to 1929, with the exception of a few wedding dresses and some special stage costumes. Many were the innovations introduced by Patou at
the time which still hold good today. Possibly the most important new look to emerge at this time was the Patou

sweater. His fascination with the possibilities of this garment, until then the province of elderly ladies, school children, fishermen and Chanel's English sporting boyfriends, had been aroused when he started to design Suzanne Lenglen's sporting wardrobe.

They were conceived along strictly practical lines, short-sleeved or long, always satisfying both the demands of sport and of chic. These Patou cardigan sweaters appeared in a variety of subtle colours. At first they were plain, or simply banded in navy and white, but he then started to use the monogram device, either his own characteristic JP or that of his client. He declared that a 'monogram will always add distinction to a very plain sweater.'

By 1924, Patou's sweaters had come a long way from their tennis-court antecedents and had become subtly intricate. The best that Patou designed at this time were inspired by the cubists and were balanced blocks of colour placed rhythmically on predominantly V-necked sweaters. Even after fifty years, these are timeless.

He then started to show twinsets, extending the cubist idea into coordinating sweaters and cardigans and also developing beautifully balanced stripes. In designing these and popularizing them in the resorts, as well as in Paris, he virtually launched the knitting industry on a mass market as opposed to hand-knit scale. Time and time again many of Patou's cubist blocks and subtle stripings crop up in today's designer collections.

In 1924 Patou invented sweater dressing. He added printed silk scarves to match the sweaters, and then teamed them with pleated crêpe-de-chine skirts, with coordinating print. *Les riens* – the bag or the hat – would often pick up and emphasize the predominant theme. This dressing concept became the rage, and lasted with variations until the end of the twenties. Every season, Patou would produce a winner, a 'Ford' sweater that would be worn in its hundreds, and copied for the mass market in its thousands. According to *Sweater News*, an American trade magazine, the winner in summer 1925 was Patou's navy and white graduated-stripe V-neck sweater with matching cardigan and scarf.

Much later in the summer, international café society moved south, either to the Riviera, to the Lido in Venice, or to Biarritz on the Basque coast. Biarritz was very smart in the twenties, and right through the thirties too, as the late-summer haunt of the faster members of smart society, who decamped en masse at the end of August until the middle of October in order to enjoy its rather romantic proximity to Spain. This former fishing village now had such amenities as a thoroughly modern casino for the amusement of the smart set. Biarritz society was wilder than that of Deauville. It drank more, lived faster and gambled a great deal.

Raymond Barbas, a Basque himself, first introduced his brother-in-law to Biarritz shortly after his marriage to Madeleine Patou. The rich possibilities of the town had immediately appealed to Patou. In 1924, some months after the Deauville opening, he decided it would be wise to follow his clients when they migrated south and, with a typically grand gesture, bought the old *mairie* in the middle of the little town, and refurbished it as a summer couture house, for which he designed a mid-season collection of sporting and formal clothes.

By then Biarritz was the most chic resort in Europe, patronized by King Alfonso of Spain and his Queen, Ina, one of Patou's clients. A large number of the permanent residents were Spanish, who had left behind the restrictions of life in Madrid. The fabulously wealthy South Americans who came to France each year also gravitated to Biarritz, and there also were the chic Americans, such as the Morgan twins, Thelma Furness and Gloria Vanderbilt, the English (among them the Prince of Wales), and the French, of course.

Patou loved it and he always stayed for the month of September. Even his progress south was turned to good account. He travelled with two cars: a white one with a black chauffeur for the sunny stages, and a black one with a white chauffeur for the rainy ones, an interesting eccentricity which did not pass unnoticed in the social columns.

Enjoying the racy atmosphere, and realizing that he was doing a very good mid-season business at a traditionally quiet time, Patou decided to build a permanent home in Biarritz, and he commissioned Sue and Mare to design it. Los Borritos is on a hill above Biarritz at Ustarritz, and floats like a geometric chimera of white planes at the end of an avenue of cypresses. It is open and airy, with a magnificent view beyond the swimming pool. Built at the height of Patou's success, it still stands as a reminder of the elegant simplicity that was the hallmark of anything Patou touched, of his sure and delicate taste in every aspect of twenties taste.

When the house was built, its uncompromising modernism attracted a great deal of local curiosity. Raymond Barbas remembers that the curate was one visitor – and he tore his soutane while walking in the garden. A few days later, he was astonished to find a Jean Patou couture dressbox waiting for him when he came back from mass, containing a new 'couture' soutane, with a Patou label, which he never tired of showing his parishioners.

*   *   *

The rivalry between Patou and Chanel continued, their jealousy unabated despite their differing personalities and methods of working. Their working methods are best described as the difference between organic and intellectual designing. The organic designer loves the flow and drape of cloth against the body, using the human form as a canvas on which to paint the picture he has in his mind's eye. An organic designer, such as Chanel, uses hands, pins, scissors, needles, luxuriating in the feel of the pliant wool or silk under the fingers. The intellectual designer, epitomized by Patou on the other hand, thinks; the picture is in the mind's eye, but it is an abstract idea. In thinking about his work, his thoughts concern practicality and freedom, or the pulse of his times. In Patou's case this included thought about the pared-down lines of a racing car applied to a new 'look'. Chanel cut, pinned and draped on the living model. She was an instinctive designer, and then rationalized her instincts in the form of fashion diktats afterwards. Patou, however, would think first, look around, and translate his thoughts about the contemporary world into clothes. Research, plan, design, edit.

The rivalry became so heated at one point that Patou wrote a very strong letter to Edna Woolman Chase at *Vogue*, complaining that he was receiving fewer pages of publicity than his rival. The doughty Mrs Chase was not going to take that sort of comment from anyone, and replied that since these pages were unpaid and the matter of her editors' discretion, she would have no hesitation in rewarding Patou's criticism

with no pages at all. Unwilling to antagonize the most important woman in fashion journalism, Patou wrote a letter of
apology, but he naturally continued to compete with Chanel
whenever and wherever possible.

Harry Yoxall, head of the London office of *Vogue*, was sent
to deal with Patou during another flare-up about editorial
pages and remembers in his memoirs, *A Fashion of Life*, being
ushered into the *maître*'s office. It was decorated and furnished entirely in white, he was guarded by a white borzoi
and the only article on his desk was a pearl-handled revolver.
Mr Yoxall did, however, get out alive – and carrying an
advertisement order with him.

Chanel remained a thorn in Patou's side until the end of
his career. Jealousy was part of it, and this rivalry was fanned
by Chanel's much publicized aesthetic forays into ballet costume design, and her patronage of the arts in general, aided
by the always useful Misia Sert. It was a general rule at *Vogue*
and at *Harper's Bazaar* that Chanel and Patou clothes should
never appear on facing pages, and, similarly, in life, they
steered clear of each other. Patou may have dressed the 'free
woman', but in Coco Chanel, he made an exception to his
general liking for bright, independent women. He didn't like
her, and he always made it perfectly clear.

When asked by Baron de Meyer in an interview in *Harper's
Bazaar* whether he felt that women made better dressmakers
than men, Patou took his opportunity to get back at Chanel:
'I don't believe,' said Patou, 'that to belong to what is termed
le beau sexe is an advantage for a dressmaker, especially not
for a *chef de maison*. Particularly so,' he told de Meyer, obviously referring to Chanel, 'when the *patronne* is young,
good-looking and chic. She will, as a matter of course, while
designing her new models, consider the effect she herself
would produce in these same gowns. To my way of thinking,'
Patou said, 'this is detrimental to good dressmaking, for there
is more than one type of woman to consider. Women's styles
and women's figures vary considerably and all of these should
be taken care of.

'The models designed by men,' he continued, 'seem to me
to be more to the point and to fulfil their purpose better. After
all, for whom do women dress? Isn't it men,' asked Patou,
mischievously, knowing that it would infuriate Chanel, 'that

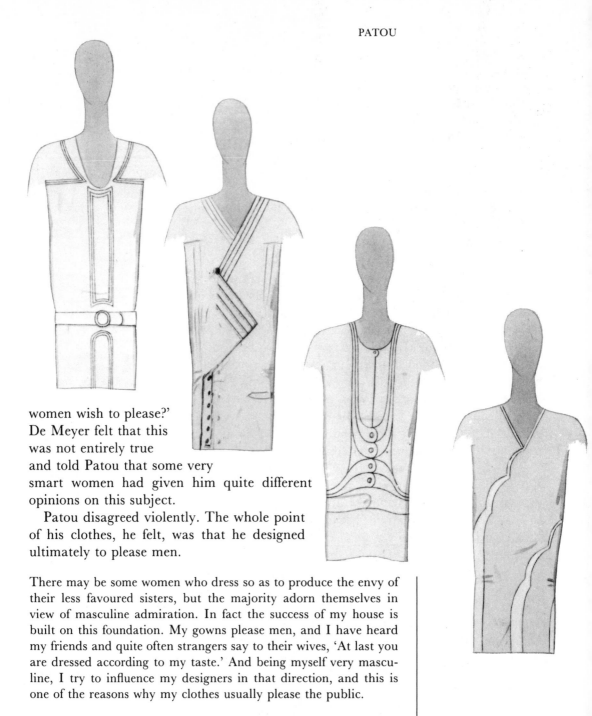

women wish to please?'
De Meyer felt that this
was not entirely true
and told Patou that some very
smart women had given him quite different
opinions on this subject.

Patou disagreed violently. The whole point
of his clothes, he felt, was that he designed
ultimately to please men.

There may be some women who dress so as to produce the envy of
their less favoured sisters, but the majority adorn themselves in
view of masculine admiration. In fact the success of my house is
built on this foundation. My gowns please men, and I have heard
my friends and quite often strangers say to their wives, 'At last you
are dressed according to my taste.' And being myself very masculine, I try to influence my designers in that direction, and this is
one of the reasons why my clothes usually please the public.

Unlike the situation now prevalent in international fashion
design, Paris couture was dominated by heterosexual men in
the first two decades of the century. Jacques Worth, Doucet,

LE COIN
DES
SPORTS

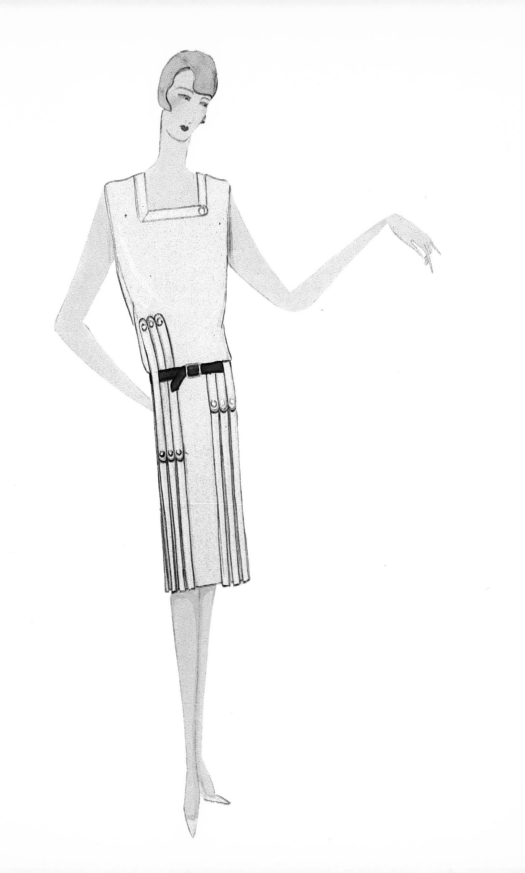

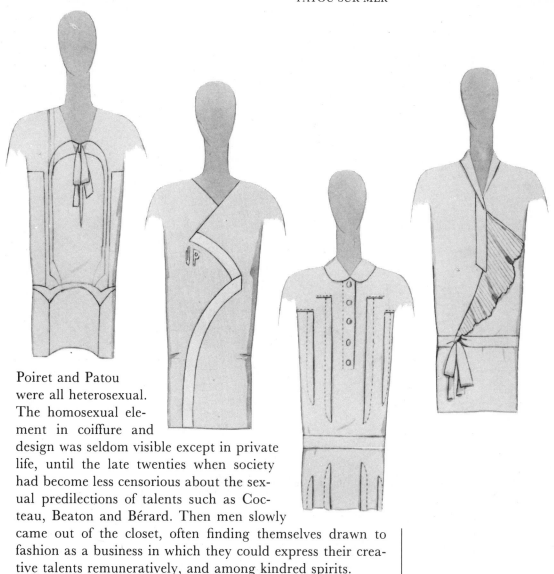

Poiret and Patou were all heterosexual. The homosexual element in coiffure and design was seldom visible except in private life, until the late twenties when society had become less censorious about the sexual predilections of talents such as Cocteau, Beaton and Bérard. Then men slowly came out of the closet, often finding themselves drawn to fashion as a business in which they could express their creative talents remuneratively, and among kindred spirits.

Just as Patou dressed the elegant, intelligent woman to appeal to men, so did Chanel. Both of them were working to the same end: to abolish frills, to make clothes that were easy to wear, that didn't swamp the personality. Their design language was similar. Chanel's was more sinuous, Patou's more architectural. Both were of their time in all their inconsistencies, their fascination with new ideas and their liking of the good life.

Their rivalry was intense, however. If Chanel designed

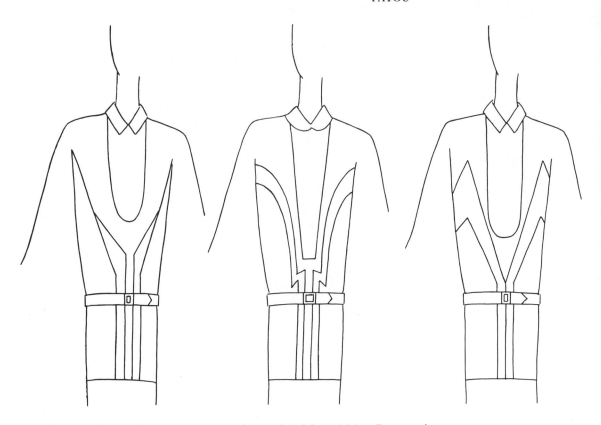

clinging beige jersey dresses, trimmed with rabbit, Patou designed navy dresses with cubist pleats, trimmed with white piqué. The rivalry no doubt stimulated them – certainly when Patou dropped his hemlines in 1929, creating a sensation, he did it partly in response to Chanel's ever-shorter little black dresses.

The merits of the two designers were hotly debated by smart women, but perhaps the writer Anita Loos should have the last word. A client of both, she was very definite about her preference: 'Patou,' she said, just before she died in 1981, 'made Chanel look like a milliner. He revolutionized the way women dress ... before him it was all ruffles and flounces and after it was clean and elegant. Chanel was nowhere, compared with him.'

* * *

Barely visible on this sunny mid-twenties horizon was a small, dark shadow that would grow as the decade drew to its close.

Patou had everything he had wanted and worked for. A huge
business run by able colleagues and devoted staff. A measure
of personal fame, and an acknowledgement by his peers of his
supremacy at the top of the couture tree. He was an international success and an international name. Patou's gambling, however, had grown from an amusing diversion into
an overwhelming preoccupation that mounted in intensity
with his losses. 'It is safe to say that Patou wagered and lost
more money in the casinos of France and Monte Carlo than
any gambler in history,' Elsa Maxwell said. 'I know the
apocryphal stories of sums lost at the chemin de fer tables,
but I never saw a plunger in Patou's class.'

Fleeting friendships with innumerable pretty women were
not enough to satisfy his appetite for living dangerously, but
to begin with he managed, as Elsa Maxwell appreciated, to
turn his gambling to good account.

Patou was a press agent's dream, but in the final analysis he was
a better publicity man for himself than anyone he could have hired.
He promoted his personality with an intuitive dramatic flair that
even turned his weakness for gambling into a business asset. One
night at Biarritz, when he was taking an appalling beating at chemin
de fer, I tried to tell him he was a sucker to continue playing for
high stakes while luck was running against him. Patou cut me short
with a laugh. 'Each million I lose here sells two million francs'
worth of clothes,' he said. 'Relax, *chérie*, it's what you Americans
call spreading goodwill.'

Elsa Maxwell felt it was something much more subtle than
that. Watching Patou gamble was, she felt, a lesson in applied
psychology. 'His strong handsome face was impressive except
for the flicker of a sardonic smile when a croupier swept away
his bet. When he won, he rarely looked at the pile of chips
pushed towards him. He was actually following with his eyes
the figure of a woman as she walked across the room. An
interest that was more real than affected. I know,' said Elsa,
'that I sound like an infatuated schoolgirl, but Patou radiated
an aura of glamour that was irresistible to women. His ex-
cessive gambling, affairs and extravagance were the magnets
that drew women to his salon on the pretext of buying
clothes.'

In Biarritz, Patou spent only an hour or so a day in the

salon. The rest of his time was devoted to entertaining streams of society guests at large lunch and dinner parties, driving or taking one of the motorboats to other parties up and down the coast, and to gambling. Patou always arrived at the casino after midnight, whether in Biarritz, Nice or Monte Carlo, and rarely left before dawn. He played with other committed gamblers – the Aga Khan, the Duke of Westminster and, above all, Madame Ephrussi, born a Rothschild and, by common consensus, a rival for Patou's title of the heaviest gambler on the coast.

Mrs Jean Nash, one of Patou's biggest clients, and known in the American press as 'The Most Extravagant Woman in the World', took the lid off this high gambling milieu in a sensational article in a New York newspaper, illustrated by a Tigre cartoon of the most obsessive gamblers on the international circuit: Madame Ephrussi, André Citröen, the motor manufacturer who could lose the equivalent of 'sixty cars a night', the Aga Khan, sarcastically described by Mrs Nash as 'the spiritual leader of millions', Henri Letellier and his aide-de-camp Erskine Gwynn, Jefferson Davis Cohn, the railroad magnate, and of course, Jean Patou. 'There are a few evening gowns gone west,' Mrs Nash reported Patou saying, as he threw packets of ten thousand franc notes across the table.

Parties occupied a great deal of Patou's time and these were really magnificent affairs. 'The first time I saw Chaplin was when he gave an unforgettable one-man show in Biarritz in 1928,' said Elsa Maxwell.

Jean Patou had hired a fleet of motorboats to take a party of guests to a bullfight at Bayonne, but the excursion was cancelled by a violent hurricane that blew up suddenly. The storm knocked out the electric lights and several women showed signs of panic as the wind and the rain mounted in fury until Charlie Chaplin took charge of the situation.

Chaplin told Maxwell that it was 'nonsense to sit around like this, let's amuse ourselves, play something from *Carmen* and I'll take it from there.' Elsa recalled:

With no preparation, Chaplin proceeded to give an enthralling pantomime of a bullfight in the flickering candlelight. He impersonated in turn a frenzied spectator, the bull, a picador, a gored horse and the matador. Each characterization was so perfect and the continuity had revealed such dramatic purity that there was a collective gasp when he made the matador's final thrust at the bull. With a subtle shrug, Chaplin abruptly changed the mood and improvised a tragic triangle in which a husband murdered his wife and her lover, and then committed suicide. Chaplin's artistry held us spellbound for three hours by the watch. It was not until he had finished that we realized the hurricane had long since subsided.

Despite such divertissements, Patou turned more and more to the gambling tables for excitement, his losses growing larger until they finally damaged all that he had worked to create. In the end, his gambling became more important to Patou than clothes and flirtations with the women who wore them – two interests that he combined, notably when he hired the Dolly Sisters in 1924 as mannequins.

The Dolly Sisters were a phenomenon. Identical, rather oriental in appearance, Rosie and Jenny divided their working lives almost equally between being music-hall stars, doing little but walk on and off stage in a succession of superbly extravagant clothes, and being kept by a series of rich protectors, of whom the most generous was probably the department store tycoon, Gordon Selfridge, who set them up in a penthouse above his department store in London.

The Dollys, as they were always known, were extremely expensive, as the description of the wardrobe Patou made for a promotional trip to America in spring 1924 reveals. The visit had been planned by Patou and Raymond Barbas to pave the way for Patou's own visit, the only one he ever made to America, later that year. For the Dollys, Patou created over two hundred outfits, and, in addition, designed everything that went with them, from knickers to hair slides. As Patou's *mannequins de ville*, it was the Dollys' business to publicize the full spectrum of Patou's activities. Two-hour fittings at Patou every day for two months had been necessary to assemble the collection. Sometimes one Dolly went, sometimes the other, an unusual advantage of being identical twins. A fashion journalist, who wrote under the name of Angelina in *Theatre Review*, noted with amazement that:

Two hundred or more of dresses, evening wraps, coats, *tailleurs* they

77

have brought over, to say nothing of lingerie, shoes, about one hundred and fifty pairs, hats, accessories and jewellery.

An interesting mode in *tailleurs* was the model that Patou had designed for them – strictly tailored short wrap-around skirts and seven-eighth length coats, in rough materials in tan or pepper-and-salt mixtures. With them went heavy white satin blouses of hip length which buttoned straight down the front with a row of small round satin-covered buttons, and a little boutonnière of gardenias or red roses, according to the *tailleur*.

The Dollys stepped out with slender lacquered canes to match. One is reminded of that more recent cane-carrying member of the smart set – Bianca Jagger.

'Don't forget those canes,' exhorted Angelina. 'The Dollys have them in colours to match or contrast with different suits, and they have a like affection for the buttonhole.' She was amazed to see a top drawer 'all laid out like a flower-bed, with gardenias and camellias in white and pink and red . . . roses . . . carnations . . . narcissus, both white and yellow'.

Pausing a moment for breath, Angelina gushed, 'What shall I tell you about next?' She haltingly went on to describe 'What might reasonably be called a jerkin of red leather, bright but yet dark. . . . It is embroidered in narrow gold braid and gold thread, and has an accompanying hat of red leather, gold-embroidered. It is worn over a gold-embroidered white crêpe-de-chine slip with a pleated skirt, and the cap sleeve showing at the top of the arm softens the leather armhole.'

Angelina found the Dolly lingerie as thrilling as the rest of their clothes. 'Fancy, they fit lingerie over in Paris just the way they do clothes.' 'This nightgown I now have on,' Rosie Dolly told her, 'took two fittings and many days to finish.'

The Dolly dressing gowns were exclaimed over, too. 'As on a man's shirt, there is a little tab at the end of the vest part on which is embroidered their names in script.' Even their handkerchiefs came in for close scrutiny, being in sheerest linen with rolled hems, in deep blue, deep rose, maize, violet or green, with a tall monogram on them in one corner, contrasting not matching the colour of the linen. 'For evening, they carry the same handkerchief, but all in white,' Angelina finished.

The Dollys' visit to America helped Patou promote himself as a major Paris couturier in a country which, at the end of 1924, was still buying far more Chanel clothes than Patou. And yet he was much more American in his attitude than Chanel, and it was naturally a source of tremendous irritation that America continued to resist his designs. It was partly for this reason that he conceived with the Dolly sisters the best publicity stunt of his entire career, and one which was to put him on the fashionable American map so firmly that the name 'Patou' became synonymous in the minds of many American women with 'Paris couture'.

5

Venus and Diana

French clothes were enormously popular in America generally, but Patou until the mid-twenties was not as well known
as Chanel or Lanvin. They not only sold in such temples of
high fashion as Bergdorf Goodman, but they were also patronized by the Seventh Avenue wholesalers, who made
cheaper copies for the mass market. A wholesaler might buy
over £100,000's worth of designs from one house a season,
and many of the salespeople could make over £10,000 in
commission in a year. Obviously, Patou had to do something
to entice the Americans away from the competition. Edna
Woolman Chase, editor of American *Vogue* at the time, takes
up the story.

One day, one of Patou's American clients, watching a mannequin
pass, sighed wistfully and then remarked impatiently, 'Yes, but how
is it going to look on me? French and American women are built so
differently. They're smaller and rounder, we're long-legged and
lean. How to know?'
   It swept over Patou like a flash. Murmuring something about the
exquisite desirability of both the rounded French Venus and the
slender American Diana, he hurried to his office and set the wheels
spinning.

   At this point, Philippe Ortiz, Paris Director of *Vogue* and
a good friend of Patou's, had the idea of importing some
American mannequins, maintaining that American society
women who visited Paris regularly liked his clothes, but the
Americans who stayed at home did not really know his name.
But, if they did, the Seventh Avenue wholesalers would be
encouraged to beat a path to his salon.
   To take American mannequins to Paris would be a won-

Jean Patou (left) in an
uncharacteristically reflective
mood. *Patou*

At a party in Paris (below) in the early thirties. *Patou*

Deauville, the mid-thirties (bottom). Patou has aged
visibly. *Patou*

The Patou boutique at Deauville

Leap-frogging on the sands. A group of models demonstrates
the practicality of Patou's bathing suits. *Patou*

Josephine Baker (above), the toast of Paris in the 1920s, wears one of Patou's later fantasy dresses. *Patou*

The Dolly Sisters (top right), Rosie and Jenny, in identical Patou ensembles. *Patou*

Pola Negri (right) in a late-twenties Patou evening gown. *Patou*

The 'cocktail bar' (far left) where perfumes could be sampled and tested

El Ambrose (left) in a typical late Patou dance gown

Patou and his American mannequins en route for Paris (below)

Sarah Bernhardt (above) inspired this
Harper's Bazaar Patou gown; (left) another
Patou evening dress in a drawing by Jean
Cocteau

robe de Patou

Black organza for an evening
wrap and underneath a plain
black crêpe, seen as through a
glass darkly.

To protect themselves against the ever-active copyists, many couturiers, inspired by Madelaine Vionnet's example, photographed their clothes, back, front and sides, and then registered the designs (below). These pictures provide a marvellous record of Patou's collections. Here, a late day outfit from the winter 1925 collection, showing the curves that were beginning to replace the geometric angularity of his pure cubist period

Slightly more formal lines, discreet pleats and the JP monogram show in Patou's Parisian look (above)

Typical geometric shapes
distinguish this casual Patou
ensemble from the mid-1920s
(below)

The House of Patou in its Biarritz heyday

Raymond Barbas and Edna Woolman Chase
photographed in the early fifties when Barbas was
president of the Chambre Syndicale de la Couture

derful way of showing how Patou's clothes would look on typical American figures. Neither Patou nor Ortiz realized that importing Americans to the capital city of fashion would provoke a storm of publicity in newspapers and magazines all over the world. Overnight, Patou became the most talked-about Paris couturier in the world, and probably the most controversial, certainly in that golden year of 1925. The fact that this happened is, in itself, a barometer of the status accorded to couture at the time, and the relative sangfroid with which it is regarded now.

In November 1924, Patou made his move. He simply advertised in the New York daily press. Fashionable New York was amused and astonished to read the following advertisement:

MANNEQUINS WANTED FOR PARIS

Jean Patou, the Parisian couturier, desires to secure three ideal types of beautiful young American women who seriously desire careers as mannequins in his Paris atelier. Must be smart, slender, with well-shaped feet and ankles and refined of manner. Sail within three weeks. Attractive salary proposition, one year's contract and travelling expenses both ways. Selection to be made at the offices of *Vogue*, 14th Floor, 10 West 44th Street. Apply Friday morning 10.00 to 12.30.

It is difficult now to credit the furore this caused. Before Patou's Americans, couture mannequins in Paris had always been French. Of course, there were photographic and show models in New York, but most of them regarded themselves as 'semiprofessional'. They were resting actresses, soubrettes in revues that opened and closed just as rapidly or artists' models. But five hundred of them queued up outside the *Vogue* offices that Friday morning. Seeing how lovely many of them were, Patou decided to choose six rather than three; about a hundred 'semifinalists' were asked to return to the Ritz ballroom a few days later.

The jury that greeted the hundred girls at the Ritz comprised some expert spotters – Edna Woolman Chase, and Condé Nast, her publisher, owner of both *Vogue* and *Vanity Fair*; Elsie de Wolfe, the decorator and international socialite; and the *Vogue* photographer Edward Steichen. When the girls arrived they were told to form a line and walk slowly round the room as if they were showing a dress. They had all dressed as smartly as possible in current American fashions from local designers such as Travis Banton and Lucile. These clothes were very different to the streamlined Paris look. The American designers had not abandoned waists and hips and were still designing full-skirted, tight-waisted creations, with abundant trimmings.

According to Dinarzade, one of the hopefuls, Patou appeared to be more interested in feet and ankles than in anything else. If they passed inspection, he then looked at the girl's hips, or rather for the lack of them.

Patou now narrowed the choice down to six. One of them was Dinarzade, an ex-actress named Lillian Farley, *née* Mulligan, from Knoxville, Tennessee, who had become famous for showing Lucile's 'picture dresses'. These were so called because opulent American society matrons like Mrs Vanderbilt always wore Lucile dresses when they had their portraits painted. Patou asked Dinarzade, through Georges Bernard, 'My dear, will you please tell me why you dress so? Look at that! A tight-fitting bodice when the mode says the line must be straight! You are most attractive, but certainly you are not chic. But you could be made so.' Apart from her picture-frock past, Dinarzade was an unusual choice for Patou to make for she was much taller than the average petite Patou type. As he was in the throes of opening the Coin des Sports and designing sportswear for coltish twenties girls, Patou was looking for willowy mannequins who would be able to break into a stride rather than glide down the catwalk.

For a salary of $40 a week, and the prospect of becoming famous as a Patou mannequin, the Paris proposition was extremely attractive. And with a Patou ensemble available to the mannequins for as little as $25, Dinarzade and the five other American girls whom Patou chose were considered very lucky. They were six very different types of American beauty. Carolyn was a tiny perfect version of the 'small' American woman. Edwina was taller with blonde hair worn in a long bob, an ex-dancer from George White's *Scandals*. Rosalind was a tall Scandinavian type who had already made a career as a photographer's model. Josephine was a flaming redhead, a colour just then becoming fashionable for the first time in over a century thanks to Elinor Glyn and the 'It' girl; and Dorothy was a natural ash blonde, slightly plump. She promised to watch her diet and take off some extra pounds.

Patou sailed back from America before his mannequins and the week following his departure was completely taken up with interviews and posing for publicity photographs. These appeared in American magazines with articles telling the world how six American girls were going to France to show the French mannequins how to model clothes. Baron de Meyer himself took a photograph of Dinarzade in a beautiful beaded evening gown from Patou, which was shaded in tones of coral pink deepening to old rose.

In France the news that Patou was importing American models led to pointed comments in the press along the lines of 'taking the bread from the mouths of the French mannequins'. Patou became worried that the whole project might backfire and sent the faithful Georges Bernard to board the *Savoie* before the girls landed, to warn them to be discreet. They eventually became very friendly with their French colleagues.

Arriving at Le Havre, the girls were surprised to be met not only by Patou, Raymond Barbas and other members of Patou's equipage, but also by the full panoply of press photographers and even some members of Parisian society, curious to catch a glimpse of these exotic imports.

Patou had organized a gala lunch on the train to Paris, and he took the opportunity of warning the girls about some of the pitfalls they might meet as mannequins in Paris, as Dinarzade remembers: 'Girls, now we must talk seriously,' he cautioned them via his 'English eyes and ears' Raymond Barbas. 'Paris is very, very dangerous for young girls like you. Here there are many people with bad characters. I expect you to be sensible. Above all, you must not go out with those gigolos who hang around the Ritz and who are just wastrels.'

The American girls were enchanted with their first sight of Paris, and their rooms in the Palais d'Orsay hotel, but not so thrilled when they found that Patou had had their connections on the telephone switchboard plugged with paper. He obviously knew what to expect with six American girls in Paris!

The morning after their arrival, they walked across the

Tuileries to the rue St Florentin. On that December morning in 1924, the girls found themselves in the brilliantly lit first-floor salon, crowded as usual with *vendeuses* all shouting instructions to one another. Every *vendeuse* wore a beige crêpe dress, and although each was made differently all bore the unmistakable Patou stamp.

They could not have arrived at Patou at a better time. The previous season, the winter 1924 collection, had been one of his most restrained and elegant, and *Vogue* had commented at the time:

Patou has become a specialist in the design of ensembles that adapt to all the circumstances of the day. The press at the showing of his collection was of the unanimous opinion that the models he presented would be bound to be classed with the best creations of the popular couture. He himself drew our particular attention to the many dresses vaguely inspired by the period 1887 to 1890.

These were in fact fluid and almost Pre-Raphaelite, often with asymmetrical pleating to give them verve and movement. As always, each collection had a dominant colour theme and, for spring 1925, this was to be a particularly subtly tinted beige, which Patou called rose-beige.

Apart from launching the new colour, Patou was planning a volte-face. He was going to move away from the ruler-straight little dresses, working on a more fluid and mobile look, centred around the controversial area of the waist.
As Patou said at the time, 'The low waistline is dying, passing by, soon to be forgotten. We are done with artistic whims and grotesqueries and are back at a real line in the silhouette of style, a normal line, beautiful because it is natural.'

Vogue picks up the story again:

Paris fashion has this spring witnessed a phenomenon the like of which has seldom, if ever, occurred in the mercurial city. It has seen style turned in a week – and by one will . . . The new Patou waistline – the nearly normal waistline – is a vast success. Some of the smartest Parisians, leaders of the fashion in the gay capital, are wearing it . . . at Ciro's, at the Ritz, and the Opéra, wherever Parisian women of elegance congregate. . . .

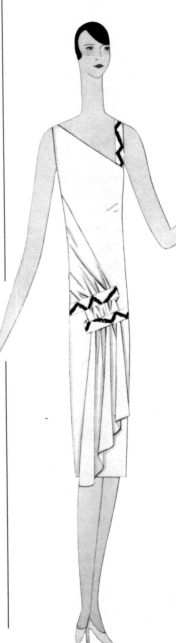

Patou's new waist was subtle, not belted, but simply indicated by movement or discreet shaping. The cut was extremely complicated: he used godets, insets, stitched-down pleats, moving panels, frills and jabots. It resulted in an extremely feminine graceful and fluid look.

The American girls were fascinated by the preparations for the new collection. Things were as always frenetic. The first sign that work had started in earnest was the closure of four out of the five interlocking first-floor salons. These then became a private studio. One of them metamorphosed into a stockroom, containing hundreds of bolts of new materials piled on trestle tables. There were sporty tweeds specially woven to Patou's designs by Linton from Scotland, fine wools, kashas, and jerseys from Rodier and J. B. Martin, printed crêpes-de-chines and silk mousseline from Bianchini Ferier in Lyons, and most precious of all, the tiny samples of beaded designs, most of them hand-embroidered to Patou's designs by White Russian émigrées.

Almost swamped by the bolts of fabric, three artists turned out detailed sketches by the dozen. These were never copied line for line, but were scrutinized for details, ideas for trimmings and interesting decorative treatments. The sketches produced in the studio were pinned to the brocaded walls of the first salon where Patou's *première*, Madam Lucile, worked. In the second salon, Patou himself received designers and craftsmen who submitted buttons, trimmings, flowers and other decorative novelties. These were particularly important in Patou's case because he liked to decorate his simple lines with a twisted piece of silk braid, or with embroidered flowers, forming a soft edge to collar or hem.

On one side of the salon, a large blackboard took up most of one wall. It was chalked off in twenty sections, with the name of a mannequin at the top of each. As a garment was decided upon, and assigned to the appropriate mannequin with a number, the number was marked underneath the name of the girl who would wear it. White chalk indicated the day dresses, red chalk the evening gowns.

The system of allocating a dress to a particular mannequin illustrates the personal approach of twenties' couturiers; they were not designing something to fit, or suit, everyone. They designed for 'types' and little was interchangeable. There were dresses and ensembles for different mannequins who represented different types of client. Every designer created some clothes for small, neat women, and others for the taller, more athletic woman. In Patou's case, this personal approach was one of the keys to his success. He refused to sacrifice what was becoming for an abstract fashion principle.

The fittings took place in the fourth salon. Here the tailors and dressmakers brought down the canvas patterns known as *toiles*. These were tried on several girls in turn until one was found who looked specially well in it. If Patou approved, they would be submitted to Madame Lucile. This was the point at which bolts of fabric were brought in and draped.

The relationship between a couturier, such as Patou, and his *première* has always been central to a classic couture house. It is the *première* who executes the designer's ideas. Between Patou and Madame Lucile, there existed a close working rapport. Together they would throw fabrics over a mannequin, pin, and drape, and cut. Patou, with his superb colour sense, and Madame Lucile had an almost telepathic understanding.

In preparation for their contribution to the spring 1925 collection, the Americans had been given their own *cabine*. It had been newly decorated with grey walls, long mirrors and an enormous make-up table running the length of the room. The girls were measured for special underwear of rose-pink crêpe-de-chine. Tiny tight pants and bodices had their names hand-embroidered across the front. Greco, the Paris shoemaker, arrived to measure them for shoes. That season, Patou chose oxblood calf Oxfords for formal and sporty clothes, beige satin pumps for day clothes, and silvery-rose brocade shoes for evening.

After the fittings came the collection. Beyond the curtain in the salons, the international set would be well represented by the American Elsie de Wolfe, wife of Sir Charles Mendl, who gave some of the most elegant parties of the twenties at her home in Versailles. Mrs Harrison Williams, often described as the world's best-dressed woman, would be there. So would Mrs Reginald Fellowes, known as Daisy. She had an extraordinarily individual style and worked with Carmel Snow on *Harper's Bazaar* in the thirties. Rothschilds, film stars such as Pola Negri, Mary Pickford, Gloria Swanson, Lya de

Putti, Louise Brooks would all attend, as well as a sprinkling of quietly elegant aristocratic Frenchwoman from the Faubourgs. The English, ranging from Lady Colefax, interior decorator and a rival hostess to Lady Cunard, to more county ladies such as Lady Abingdon or Lady Milbanke, were also invited.

The salons, now stripped of sketches and swatches, were brilliantly spotlit. Tables were set around the walls in a single line, leaving space in the centre for the mannequins to show the clothes. Before the mannequins appeared they had to pass a final inspection. Alone in the small salon, Patou sat, smoking. Madame Lucile hovered nervously in the background with Georges Bernard and Madame Louise, who directed the salons. This was a crucial moment, the knife edge, that spice of danger that Patou loved. Ultimately, it was his singular, editorial eye that really pulled the collection together, and he always did so at the last possible moment.

Patou had of course seen each outfit from the moment it had been sketched. He had chosen, or designed, many of the fabrics, bullied his suppliers into dyeing his special colours, shrieked at the trimming makers, and chosen his buttons and his corsages. But he had never seen the entire ensemble of dress, hat, bag, gloves, and, of course, girl. And this spring season of 1925 was crucially important.

After all the publicity about the American mannequins, Patou knew that it was important for his look to work for these tall, leggy girls as well as it did for the rounded French models. The collection had to live up to expectations. It was a dangerous moment. If any dress lacked a particular stamp, a neatness, a collected, illusory simplicity, then Patou rejected it, however late in the proceedings.

For the spring 1925 season, Patou added a theatrical touch, originating in the Venus and the Diana controversy. He brought both the French and the American mannequins on for their first entrance in single file, dressed only in the little *toile* wrappers they wore in the dressing room between fittings. Patou's genius for the moment triumphed again, for his demonstration that the female form, whatever the nationality, still comprised head, limbs and torso – and was all a dressmaker had to work with – caused much good-natured laughter, predisposing the audience to like the collection.

Patou had produced a supremely feminine collection in shades of rose and beige, and one that began again to show the natural shape of the female figure. The evening dresses were works of art with beautiful beaded crystal fringes, shimmering starlike sequins, with matching evening cloaks lined in exotic furs ... breischvantz, zibelline and ermine. 'For those who appreciate suppleness and mobility as complements to female grace,' *Vogue* told its readers, 'go and see the series of models in mousseline, crêpe-de-chine and crêpe georgette at Patou.' Patou had modified the strict, dropped waist, geometric-cut, and created clothes where there was a clue to the position of the natural waist.

The collection was a triumph in its fluid subtlety, apparent simplicity and effortlessness. The American buyers gasped. When the first waisted frocks appeared, they put them down as Patou's fantasies designed, as *Vogue* put it, 'to give savour to a monotonous procession of straight-lined sacks to be expected immediately thereafter. But waist followed waist, until at last it dawned on the buyers that Patou had given a new line to his entire spring collection.'

It was a huge gamble, a combination of shrewd and timely designing, as well as pure daring, and it paid off. It established Patou's name indelibly in America. Newfound success with American buyers did not mean that Patou neglected his private Parisian clients, however. After the retailers and the wholesalers had gone home, Patou devoted an afternoon to a collection for his French customers. It was much shorter, as only a certain number of models were considered appropriate for the private clientele he had built up since 1919. Several dozen new designs were added, most of them simple and conservative day and dinner dresses.

The chic Parisians were an international legend at that time, but Dinarzade was disappointed by her first sight of the fashion leaders en masse, and remembers that she was quite unprepared for the 'austere simplicity. A black dress, a black fur coat and a black felt hat. A handbag of black antelope with a jewelled crest or monogram, neutral-coloured shoes and stockings and beige sueded gloves to match.'

A touch of colour was added by the jewels and scarf, but to Dinarzade this sombre simplicity was a far cry from the pastel lace festoons of a Lucile picture frock. This cleanness

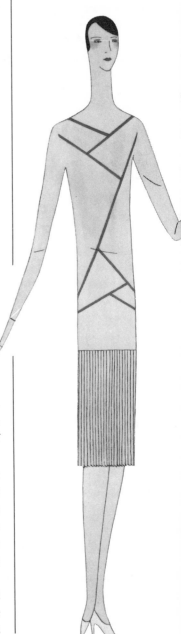

of line, so strange to American eyes, was to become more and more popular during the rest of the twenties, and the many magazine and newspaper pictures of Patou's stork-like mannequins wearing these little masterpieces of 'nothingness', was to alert the average American woman to the possibilities of simple chic, and to make a fortune for their creator.

The spring 1925 collection was the best example of Patou's impeccable sense of timing. For just as hemlines will always drop in a depression, and creep up in a boom, so too is the cut of clothes influenced by the times. In an era of affluence, of reasonably lax morals or even decadence, clothes become simpler and more youthful. It is as if women gain confidence and discard lavish display and complicated design when times are prosperous. In hard times, by contrast, such as the 1840s, the 1930s and the present era, clothes become more elaborate to reflect the need for distraction and confidence. Clothes requiring large amounts of fullness and fabric also convey an apparent, often illusory, prosperity, as if the wearer is declaring that although the times demand economy she – the exception – can be conspicuously wasteful. In creating the American Diana, Patou was exactly in the spirit of the twenties.

The start of the era of the American Diana and the French Venus, in 1925, also marked the peak of Patou's career, the beginning of a golden era, when he was assured of success at every turn.

* * *

Patou's social life at this time was as magnificently orchestrated as his public appearances. Elsa Maxwell, the court jester, saw to that. Behind her clownish mask she was a woman with driving energy, relentless ambition, little charm but boundless self-confidence. She had a real instinct for what would amuse and intrigue people, and she turned it to good use. As one of her contemporaries once remarked, when confronted with Elsa in full splendour, 'The only good thing about Elsa Maxwell is that she dresses at Patou.'

She declared, in a radio programme in America, that she not only did not like men but could never have contemplated going to bed with one – a bold statement even for that indiscreet time. She was a curious element of the flirtatious atmosphere which generally surrounded Patou, but he was perceptive enough to appreciate what she could do for his business. Like him, Elsa had a real nose for publicity as part of marketing, and in this she was years ahead of her time. She was quite prepared to manufacture the right sort of stunt, and she knew exactly how to manipulate her wide circle of acquaintances – people such as Cole and Linda Porter, Elsie de Wolfe and King Alfonso of Spain.

These people acted as shock troops in her effort to restore the sagging fortunes of Monte Carlo in the mid-twenties, and they were also extremely useful in helping her to broaden and internationalize Patou's appeal. She had been hired in 1924 to be Patou's press agent, but she became far more than that.

The publicity machine Patou had created with Elsa Maxwell's help demanded that he spend more and more time at the right places with the right people. As café society really got into its stride, Patou was to be seen, sometimes with his elegant beige whippet – which one suspects might have been chosen to harmonize with the decor – trotting at his heels, at smart openings, at the races, dining with women at Maxim's. Patou continued to foster the myth he had created, and he knew perfectly well that this was undoubtedly good for business.

He lived in an exquisite house in the rue de la Faisanderie near the Bois de Boulogne, entirely designed for him by Sue and Mare, along strictly modernist lines. For a contemporary view of the life he led at home, entertaining friends and creative associates such as Reynaldo de Luza, the Peruvian illustrator, and Boutet de Monvel, we are indebted again to Dinarzade, who went to a dinner party there just after she arrived in Paris to become a mannequin, in the spring of 1925.

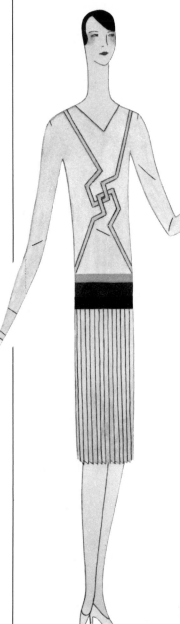

A Hispano Suiza was sent to fetch us. When we rang, the gate sprang open and we walked through a stone-paved court to the house. A footman opened the door and led us upstairs to a dressing room. Palatial was the word for this. The walls were inlaid with minute squares of gold mosaic. The bathtub and wash basin were black marble with gold faucets, a dozen heavy crystal and gold perfume bottles, graduating in size, stood on the dressing table.

In the hall, Patou's butler was shaking cocktails and the others were already in the library talking to Madame Lucile. This room opened into a large salon and there was a great feeling of space everywhere and not much furniture, but what there was of it was large and solid of the modern type. Here and there a colourful modern painting and a small but obviously very valuable collection of fine old books, leather-bound, some beautifully illuminated.

Dinarzade remembers the dining-room as being:

long and narrow, and except for the table and chairs and a long buffet at one side, there was no other furniture. There was room for twenty or more at the table, the walls were pale green and the lights were clusters of coloured globes set into the wall. The table top was mirrored and at each place there was a cobwebby oblong of linen and lace and a stunning modern silver service. The centrepiece was a huge basket of hothouse fruit and low crystal vases at each end held masses of purple orchids.

After dinner, which did not go well because Madame Lucile did not conceal her violent opposition to the idea of making clothes for the American mannequins, the company went upstairs to the studio on the top floor. This was a huge room, with dark brown lacquered walls and a tiled floor, lit by a large gilded dome in the centre. As with all Sue and Mare's interiors it looked almost austere in its simplicity, a perfect reflection of Patou's thinking.

Patou's statement in *Harper's Bazaar* concerning his belief in modernism as applied to decoration as well as dress design makes his philosophy clear:

It seems to me that the first wish of a man should be that he be 'of his own time', surrounded by decorations of his own period. I should not for a moment wish you to take me for a detractor of the past, that past which as a Frenchman and a descendant of Latins I profoundly admire.

I simply wish to share with you the opinion which I have of the importance of the development of the arts of our epoch. To be modern does not mean to upset and revolutionize. So a modern style is not a style which forgets all tradition of the past and from day to day pretends to impose a new rule. To be modern is to have the thought, the tastes, and the instincts of the epoch in which one lives. A modern art is, therefore, an art which is adapted to the tastes and to the needs of its era.

Patou believed that almost all stages of French art had been, in turn, modern epochs. 'In fact that is what has constituted its vitality and its strength. The only ones which are exceptions to this rule are the two epochs which, from the point of view of production and from the point of view of general influence, had had but a feeble result.' Patou referred here to the Empire and *Directoire* periods. 'These two epochs were never modern,' he said, 'because they never fulfilled needs and immediate demands. They have been the result of an imposed will, that of Bonaparte, that of Napoleon.'

Patou believed it was the artificial element which constituted the weakness of these two styles and rendered them inferior to many other preceding epochs which were, by contrast, vigorous. One can detect, in this didactic dismissal of the *Directoire* and First Empire styles, an echo of the philosophy of Louis Sue and André Mare, who believed that the eighteenth century had been the last era of true style, a fact reflected in their work.

I simply wish, in this little article, to make you understand the love I bear our present era, a sentiment which, after all, does not prevent my admiring all the beautiful periods of the past. Beautiful old objects or beautiful old furniture, when they are real (which is rare), are museum pieces. They should be utilized as objects of art for the education of future workers, but they should not be used. . . .

Echoes of the pronouncements of the members of the Bauhaus are evident in this statement, and this is unsurprising, for Patou must have visited the Exposition des Arts Décoratifs in 1925. Two of his sequinned evening dresses were on display as part of the French couture exhibit, and while looking at examples of art and architecture from all over Europe, Patou may well have been influenced by the work and the fundamental philosophy of the Bauhaus, then acquiring a place in avant-garde thinking.

Patou added that he believed a beautiful epoch was one in which each thing had its place, in which:

Each element contributes to the formation of a very homogeneous whole. We are not really at ease and we do not feel completely at home except in the midst of modern machinery. This latter has been perfected to the point of attaining real beauty in which the style of the epoch asserts itself. Beauty on the other hand is always in formation and in evolution, but beauty just the same. Who amongst us is not sensitive to the continuous lines, the balance, in the models of beautiful automobile coachmaking? There is no object which possesses a graceful sweep more obvious than that of a racing boat in which each outline is minutely studied and calculated so as to form a flexible whole. The eye follows these forms with pleasure and finds therein even a certain voluptuousness.

There is a clue in Patou's appreciation of the aesthetics of the automobile and of the influence of the Futurists, particularly Marinetti, to his thinking. The Futurist movement had in fact really been stopped short by the First World War, but its influence would pervade much twenties' thought. An echo of Marinetti's *Initial Manifesto of Futurism*, 20 February 1909, can be found in Patou's remarks about cars, as, for instance, when Marinetti declared that: 'The world's splendour has been enriched by a new beauty: the beauty of speed. A racing motorcar, its frame adorned with great pipes like snakes with explosive breath . . . a roaring motorcar which seems to run on shrapnel, is more beautiful than the Victory of Samothrace.'

Patou was less extreme when he equated the flowing lines of a racing boat with a certain voluptuousness, but his thinking, in common with many of his contemporaries, must nevertheless have been coloured by these influences. 'Let us live, as far as our means permit, in harmony with our life,' said Patou. 'May our furniture, our clothing, the machinery we use, be quite of the same family. It is thus that we shall build ourselves a personal home, representative of our epoch, but also of our minds.' Patou was talking about his house, but he was also talking about the guiding principle behind every couture dress he designed.

Patou was exactly of his time in believing harmony of design could be extended into every aspect of life, including dress, decoration, transport and art. The twenties has been much fêted as the last great era of total design. It is interesting to reflect that by the time the thirties had established itself as an era of fantasy, ephemerality, rooted in a shallow appreciation of influences as diverse as surrealism and the rococo, Patou's star had begun to decline. He was not a dilettante, he adhered to the principle of harmony – and this is possibly one of the reasons he found himself so out of tune with thirties' rhythms.

6

Joy

Around 1924, the more percipient couturiers had begun to realize that there were tremendous opportunities for them to diversify into areas related to dress, and that their *griffes*, the signatures which had been established with such care and effort, would be just as potent an inducement to buy accessories as they had been for clothes. Accessories were an obvious development, but scent, at first, was not. When the couturiers discovered how successful René Coty had become by marketing scent for the masses, however, they began to turn their attention to this, realizing that there were many women who could not buy designer clothes, but coveted a good label on something, even if it were just a small bottle.

Looking back to the twenties from today's era of readily available perfume, either cheap or expensive, corner chemist or duty free, it seems strange how scarce the commodity was before the development of synthetics. Scent had been the province of a few specialist blenders who could brew their natural perfumes only in tiny quantities. Lilac, rose and geranium were the natural smells which the Edwardians so loved. Family-run businesses such as Guerlain kept their recipes a closely guarded secret, generation after generation, and still do.

Before synthetic perfume, scent was a question of individual 'nose' and knowhow rather than laboratory formula. Very few women could afford to wear anything but scented water and even now a superb new scent is still referred to as a 'Guerlainade', a tribute to the family that has produced a superb nose and a series of thoroughbred scents for the last six generations.

The introduction of coal tar or aniline dyes in the 1860s

enabled the creation of synthetic or laboratory scents which could be made in the large quantities demanded by mass marketing, and, because the scents could be scientifically formulated, they were more stable than their predecessors. The first person to take advantage of these developments was René Coty. Having produced some mass-market scent before the First World War, he had trouble distributing it through the large stores. He then commissioned the great glass designer René Lalique to design a distinctive bottle that would add glamour to the product – and Bon Marché, the great Paris emporium, appreciating the appeal of these beautiful bottles, bought in quantity. René Coty's fortune was made, and good packaging had helped.

Paul Poiret was the first couturier to realize the possibilities of this market, but he missed the essential point when he did not add his own label to Rosine, thus not capitalizing on his name. It was a limited success for this reason. Three years later, the enormous popularity of Coty's Chypre, Houbigant's Quelques Fleurs and Guerlain's Mitsouko gave couturiers food for thought.

Madame Lanvin hit the jackpot first with Arpège launched in 1923. Chanel, after several false starts, launched Number 5 (her fifth attempt to launch a blockbuster) in 1925. With the collaboration of Raymond Barbas, who concerned himself with this side of the business, Patou had been seeking a classic scent long before he touched the nerve of thousands of women, three generations of them now, with Joy.

In 1924 he had launched three perfumes which he typically explained as representing the three aspects of a love affair. Amour-Amour, Que Sais-Je and Adieu Sagesse. All were fruity florals typical of the tastes of the time. And, typical of Patou's approach to merchandizing, they were blended to suit three different types of women. Amour-Amour, a heavy, seductive scent was destined for smouldering brunettes. Que Sais-Je, lighter and more flowery, for blondes, and Adieu-Sagesse, spicy, slightly tart, for redheads. Neat copy, an amusing idea, but none of these scents was distinctive enough to become a classic.

In 1925 came a completely different scent, with a concept far ahead of its time. Le Sien was the first unisex perfume. 'Sport is the territory where men and women are equal,'

HUILE DE CHALDÉE

hiver comme été

votre peau

n'a plus rien à craindre
du soleil

Méfiez-vous du soleil d'hiver dans la montagne : la réverbération sur la neige en aggrave les effets.

L'HUILE DE CHALDÉE
vous donna cet été le beau hâle bronzé dont vous étiez si fière. Elle vous protègera des coups de soleil
et du froid
des
altitudes...

HUILE
DE
CHALDÉE

JEAN PATOU
PARIS

JEAN PATOU
PARFUMEUR

Le Service Typographique

Patou explained in the launch publicity. 'With sports clothes being sober and practical, a very feminine perfume would strike a false note. Le Sien is a perfume with a more masculine note. I have created, in this healthy, fresh, outdoors mood, a perfume which suits men, but which also goes very well with the personality of the modern woman, who plays golf, smokes and drives her motorcar at 120 kilometres an hour.'

A good idea, and innovative, but Patou still had not touched that elusive 'nerve' that sets one scent quite apart from all the rest.

Downstairs at rue St Florentin he installed a cubist cocktail bar with a waiter where scents could be tried and mixed, just as his clients might try a Manhattan or a Sidecar. The bar was designed in burr walnut and chrome by Sue and Mare, who also designed a miniature version which contained the trial samples. Right at the beginning, Patou had taken a leaf out of Coty's book and commissioned superb packaging and bottles, all from Sue and Mare.

To begin with, all Patou's bottles had a pineapple-shaped stopper, his 'signature', just as the dove in flight was the original signature of Lanvin. Later, he sold bottles in leather cartridge cases, designed by Jeanne Toussaint of Cartier in the form of cigarette lighters, or grouped together in modern-istic *minaudières*. Patou realized that packaging was an im-portant factor in the success of any perfume, for women were more attracted to the idea of buying bottles that would look appealing grouped together on their dressing tables, than to decanting the perfume into sprays.

The concept and the blending of Joy in 1926 was an inspira-tion which is still paying out more than handsome dividends nearly sixty years later. This elusive fragrance did not, how-ever, enter the world without the assistance of an unlikely midwife in the form of Elsa Maxwell. She and Patou together created and marketed Joy, one of the handful of truly great perfumes.

Patou and Elsa had a mutual regard, even fondness, for each other, despite Elsa's views on men. She seems to have admired his incandescent effect on women, referring to him slightly wistfully, or possibly sarcastically, as 'that Hercules'. Underneath the glitter, they were both shrewd, professional and always ready to experiment – anything to gain some column inches from an escapade of one sort or another. Their cooperation resulted not only in magnificent parties in Biarritz and Monte Carlo, but also in something more lasting than star-studded guest lists – Joy.

It is ironic that Patou is now remembered chiefly by his perfume. Nearly everyone knows of Joy, whether they are interested in fashion or not, and they remember it and the name Patou because of the brilliant marketing strategy Elsa Maxwell conceived in 1926. Joy is always recalled as being the most expensive perfume in the world, and makes a fortune for Patou's descendants by trailing a cloud of extravagance and mystique with it wherever it is sold or whoever wears it. At first, however, Joy was of doubtful promise.

Patou took Elsa Maxwell with him to Grasse, still the centre of the scent industry, early in 1926 to work with a perfumier on mixing a new scent. Patou knew he needed something absolutely outstanding because he had not yet captured the imagination of the worldwide perfume market whose existence Chanel and Lanvin had already demonstrated. The two of them, each with the extraordinary instinct for what would 'go' in café society and among leading women everywhere, were consciously trying to find a winner.

'We tried everything . . . everything the *parfumeur* could think of, and nothing was right,' Elsa Maxwell recounted in her autobiography. 'Finally, he gave up in despair telling us he had run out of new perfumes to offer us. Almost giving up in frustration, he produced one last smell made up from a blend of the most precious rose and jasmine essences.'

Telling them that this particular blend was far too expensive ever to be commercially viable acted instantly on Miss Maxwell and Patou. They practically cried 'Eureka' in unison, swiftly overruling the suggestion that they might dilute the pure essence to make the perfume cheaper. 'Nonsense,' they apparently exclaimed as one.

Elsa Maxwell always claimed that she it was who thought up the unbelievably potent line of advertising copy, enduringly bald in its appeal to the upwardly mobile as the continuing success of Joy has proved. Joy will always be 'The most expensive scent in the world'. Whichever one of them dreamed up the phrase does not really matter. The line was a stroke of real genius, and Joy is still one of the top five international scents. As usual Patou was quick to air his views about how he thought perfume affected his clients in particular, and women in general.

'Perfume is one of the most important accessories of a woman's dress,' he was telling American newspaper readers in 1927, via the nationwide NEA syndication service to which he was a regular contributor. 'It is astonishing how, of late years, the perfume industry has grown and it was somewhat a matter of surprise when, not so long ago, couturiers started dealing in perfume which, until then, seemed to be something totally alien to their business.'

Patou thought that a woman rather welcomed the intrusion, as he put it, of her couturier in the realm of the *parfumeur*, and believed that women realized that it was prompted by a desire on his part to perfect the ensemble. He believed that the sense of smell had as much importance to the world as those of sight, hearing and touch, and that, this being the case, a well-dressed woman should 'flatter all senses agreeably'. Through the span of sixty years, an echo of Patou's personality impinges on our consciousness and we can almost see the smile as he holds forth about his complete woman.

To Patou, *les riens* and the scents were all part of what he saw as his life's purpose. Tireless in his approach to running his business, Patou was an artist where women were concerned. He cared, and this is perhaps the fundamental reason for his success with a client list that ranged from *grandes dames* to sports stars, film stars to well-brought-up brides such as the Princesse de Broglie, the Visconte di Modrone or Barbara Hutton (who walked up the aisle in one of his wonderfully dramatic but simple white silk satin wedding dresses). They felt that he really liked women and to turn them out looking better than they had ever looked was what mattered most to him.

This is why Patou went to so much trouble mixing perfumes, mixing dyes, stripping down his designs to the essentials, so that the character of the woman who was to wear them would be emphasized rather than submerged. It is now difficult to understand this idea of glorifying women for the pleasure of the masculine eye, when so many top designers today are more interested in women as clotheshorses than as individuals.

Patou said that it hurt him just as much to meet a woman who used a perfume which did not suit her as to see her with ill-fitting clothes. 'I have often noticed,' he remarked, in 1927, 'that some otherwise very smart women are totally devoid of a discriminating sense when it came to choosing their perfumes and would select one, usually very expensive, which detracted from rather than added to their charm.' Patou believed that the skin of a blonde blended better with the essence of a flower or a perfume in which the scent of flowers predominated. Dark women, he thought, could adopt a much heavier and headier perfume, dominated by musk and ambergris.

By using more or less perfume, Patou realized that a totally different impression could be given, just as a touch more or less rouge completely changed a face. He also sounded a cautionary note, typical of his preoccupation with discipline and subtlety. 'A refined woman should banish all eccentricity from her perfume, as from her dress. She must perfume herself with the same discretion, taste and distinction that she displays in her clothes.' In other words, leave it to Patou, top to toe, and a growing number of clients did exactly that. Fashion leaders, such as Mlle Arrivabene, who married the Italian Conte Visconti di Modrone, entrusted their wedding dress, trousseau and all their accessories to Patou.

About now, the different areas of design and dress that Patou had been developing since the early twenties suddenly appeared as a perfectly conceived whole, and the client who went to Patou during this golden era felt she was being dressed by a master, a man equally as confident when he was working out an amusing little pair of lacquered beach sandals as he was when intructing his embroiderers on the precise degree of shading on an elaborately sequinned evening dress. Nothing escaped his attention, and everything he designed was masterly. Every sweater was a perfect balance of colour and form. Every evening dress had a paradoxical combination of grandeur and delicacy which meant absolute enchantment. During the second half of the twenties, with Chanel in a comparative rut and Molyneux yet to have his most successful seasons, Patou was supreme.

The heavy, clumsy design of the early twenties had been purified and lightened. The harsh geometric cut had been imperceptibly modified and streamlined to flatter the body. Patou had learnt how to construct clothes that swung easily when their wearers moved with the elastic stride popularized by Mrs Castle, but that remained pin-straight and narrow when not on the move. Most important of all, everything that Patou designed possessed an indefinable touch, as tangible as his label, that marked its origin.

The extremely exaggerated geometric cut of the middle of the decade was giving way, imperceptibly, to a prettier, easier line. The *garçonne*-type had entered her final, most refined, phase and a change was on the way, evident first in the hint of waist in his 1925 collection and then in the spring of 1927. Take, for instance, a daytime frock by Patou of heavy black crêpe, spiralling round the body to end in an asymmetric hem. *Vogue* pointed out that this deceptively simple dress illustrated the chic of applied bands, the irregular hemline for daytime, the diagonal line, the crossed neckline and, of course, the extreme distinction of black. It was a lexicon of new design ideas. The most important thing about it was that it was soft and more 'body conscious'. Worn with a small cloche, also diagonally banded, and a carelessly flung black fox, it illustrates the inexorable change that would continue and develop from 1927 until 1929 when fashion responded decisively and unforgettably to Patou's new direction.

Patou's mastery of fashion's lingua franca did not pass unnoticed by the magazines, who endorsed his designs with enthusiasm. 'The smartest clothes for spring and summer are all white or all black,' *Vogue* informed its readers in 1927. Such strict colours had been popular throughout the twenties for late afternoon and early evening dresses, sandwiched between the sporty beiges and the brilliant jewelled evening colours, but by 1927 they had begun to creep into day clothes as well. Black broadtail cut into diagonally worked coats was the smartest daytime fur, and even in sportswear Patou had begun to team the famous sweaters with plain black sports skirts. These were very much more 'dressed' and sophisticated than earlier versions.

For the spring and winter of 1927, Patou once again devised special shades: his 'New Blue', a very deep violet, was popular, and he produced a new beige tint, 'Ibis', which he used for his many-pleated jersey dresses. 'For the Country', one of

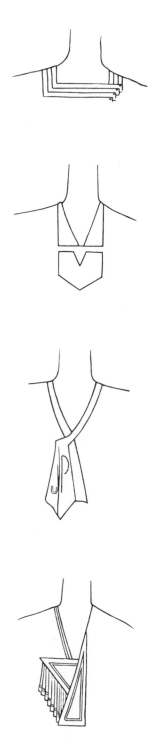

the best sellers in this collection, combined the new chic of black, in the form of a brushed-wool sleeveless sweater, with a finely pleated skirt of Ibis-coloured kasha.

It was not colour, however, that was preoccupying Patou during 1927 and 1928. He was, almost imperceptibly, continuing to alter the silhouette to one which not only had a natural waistline but which started to reflect generally the natural shape of the body. 'It is untrue that the silhouette is unchanged,' Patou told an American newspaper in November 1927. 'Although it has been widely accepted during the past few years that the trend of feminine fashion had become practically stationary . . . lines have been shifting every season, and the present mode shows a decided change from last year.

'The general idea of straight lines to follow the figure has been maintained. The modern woman demands freedom and grace and she will continue to demand them. Neither she nor her dressmaker wants to go back to the horrible old days in dress. . . .'

Patou appreciated that the well-dressed woman wanted change, but also understood that her insistence on ease of movement and lightness presented a real challenge to the couturier, because it left him with little to work with. Almost every decorative device had been eliminated and there was a depressing uniformity creeping into fashion: straight dresses, geometric seaming, plain fabrics. Beading and colour were by now the only two decorative devices left to the couturier, and designers – as well as their clients – were beginning to feel restive.

It may seem that Patou was quick to abandon the *garçonne* type, to consign her to being old-fashioned, especially as he had been largely responsible for creating her in the first place. There were good reasons for this rather dismissive attitude, one of them commercial. Patou cannot have helped but to learn from the fate of Paul Poiret. The master of the oriental look had thought that his power and influence were great enough to dictate to women, and continued to design languid oriental tea-gowns when all around him were beginning to reflect the *sportif* feeling of the mid-twenties. By 1924, Poiret was in trouble and in 1926 was bankrupt. Moving with the times, or even a little ahead of them, was one of Patou's strong points, and by 1929 he knew that the *garçonne*'s time was running out.

Women wanted, by now, to start 'dressing up' again. They had all been dressed like fourteen-year-olds, and it was time to start reintroducing those little devices that had been stripped away. After arriving at tea parties in sports suits, women now preferred to wear black velvet suits with gold lamé blouses.

Patou did not abandon sportswear altogether, but he started to relegate it to its old homes of the golf course and the tennis court. Patou was right to reflect the mood of the times, and, indeed, he had reached the point where he wanted to make more elaborate clothes again, without sacrificing the essentially sartorial liberation that sports clothes had established.

* * *

An obvious outlet for more elaborate design was offered by screen and stage, but this was one area where Patou's competitors seemed to be doing better than he, in spite of his devoted following of smart women. The growing international importance of the cinema had, by the mid-twenties, created a pantheon of international goddesses, whose mode of dress on screen, created by Lanvin, Molyneux or Chanel, was copied by women all over the world.

The studio stars, however, did go to Patou for their off-stage gowns: his Hollywood success was underlined by the 1925 headline in a show-business paper which declared that 'Lya de Putti has reached our shores. She only has twenty words of English, but she has brought a complete Patou wardrobe with her.'

The movie star clients began to be important for Patou, both in terms of the money they spent on themselves and in the publicity they generated. In 1925, for instance, Gloria Swanson spent over a quarter of a million dollars on her clothes and furs alone, much of it at Patou. Swanson was a perfect client because she was tiny, very thin and very elegant, with a quality of energy and liveliness perfectly suited to sporty clothes. The sultry Pola Negri was another favourite client of his, and whether dressed as the sportswoman or as the torrid vamp, carried off her Patou clothes with an air he appreciated.

Pola Negri is a woman of nice discernment where her clothes are concerned, and she shows it in her choice of gowns I made for her. The black georgette dress she chose is quite complicated in cut, but is still in line with the present simple fashion. It is a dress [Patou said] that was created specially for her, because there are few women who could impart that touch of originality to the sleeves which leave the arms bare, or who could carry off the unusual headband which lends the finishing touch to the gown.

People may be surprised to hear that Pola Negri looks equally well in sports clothes to which, however, she manages to impart a very personal touch. These were not meant to be worn with a turban but a turban suits Princess Mdivani's sense of beauty and does not in any way spoil the effect of the sports ensemble . . . therein lies the secret of personality.

Patou's designs, however, were neither really stagey nor obviously opulent enough to pull their weight in the cinema. Furthermore, clothes for the screen tended to lag far behind current Paris fashion, partly because the studio moguls were frightened to be seen to follow fashion in case it was too extreme for mass audiences, and partly because the long time lapse involved in making and distributing a film meant that clothes were in any case dated before the film came out.

As a result, fashion trends emerged from the movie capital itself, in parallel with Paris couture. During the twenties, Hollywood bred its own designers – men such as Travis Banton, who moved from New York couture to Hollywood, but still designed clothes that looked, even in the early thirties, as if they had been made at the beginning of the previous decade. As late as 1929, films still dressed stars as Poiret-inspired vaguely oriental vamps, and sets continued to be littered with tasselled cushions.

Patou understood why the stars wore his clothes only in private, declaring his designs to be 'the antithesis of the dress destined to be worn on the stage, which must always be more striking, more nearly of the costume type and consequently not related in any way to my style, which is one of refinement and subtlety so calculated as to be totally lost in the coarser environs of the stage or cinema screen.' One can detect a note of jealousy in this pronouncement, coming at a time when it had been announced that Chanel was to design clothes for Ina Claire in a new Broadway play.

Patou nevertheless continued to dress the screen stars – the vamps as well as an entirely different type of woman: Mary Pickford. Pickford presented a real challenge to the delicacy and refinement of Patou's design. She was so small that she bought children's clothes, and she looked much younger than her years. Even in the 1920s when she was over thirty, she was still playing fourteen-year-olds, complete with ringlets.

Privately, Mary Pickford was far from being an ingénue. A shrewd businesswoman, and a founder member of United Artists with Charlie Chaplin, she was also Hollywood's leading hostess, and had no intention of dressing like a little girl. 'When she enters my salon, I find the temptation is always great to show her the collection reserved for the young girl, but I do not believe that I am lacking in respect in stating that when she insists on seeing other models, she gives me the impression of a young girl who wants to look grown up, and who is interested in things which are not of her age,' said Patou.

'She will often choose a model and have it made in the material of another which she thinks more becoming to her personality. She has a very decided way of imparting her wishes to her *vendeuse* and needs no advice, because she is one of those rare women who knows that no matter how beautiful a girl may be, she cannot wear any and every style of dress.' In 1928, Mary Pickford bought sports clothes from Patou, and chose little dresses with what Patou called 'a swing to them'. Fluffy, intricately pieced, flowered-chiffon dresses were also·favoured.

Producing more elaborate and more showy clothes for the stars, both off stage and on, stimulated Patou to create more complex and exciting designs for his collections. Although he had made his name with his clean-cut clothes, Patou was also beginning to enjoy dressing the prettier, more fragile woman – who was beginning to overtake *la garçonne* by the end of the twenties – epitomized by another twenties woman, the professional ballroom dancer. His series of 'fluffy' printed chiffon and silk mousseline dresses in his 1927 and 1928 collections had their antecedents in a form of 'work clothes' just as his sports clothes had arisen from tennis clothes.

These women, such as Leonora Hughes and El Ambrose, were a new breed. They danced as the cabaret in such chic night spots as Le Perroquet. The genre had been invented quite accidentally one night in Paris before the First World War when Vernon and Irene Castle, out-of-work exhibition dancers, had been engaged to tango in costume at the Café de Paris.

The night before they were due to open at the Café de Paris, the Castles dressed in their own evening clothes and went to have a look at the club. Recognizing them from their photographs in the foyer, a Russian count insisted they dance for him then and there, and so they did, and a craze was born for dancers dressed similarly to their audience. It was to last until the Second World War and find its most perfect expression in the Rogers–Astaire films.

This 'non-costumed' vogue provided Patou with an interesting problem. A delicate balance had to be struck between clothes that looked as if they were 'real life' and the heightened reality that a stage performance demanded. He set out to bridge the gap between clothes for people and clothes for theatrical fantasies and in solving this problem extended his design sensibility enormously. One can see copies of the dresses he designed all the way through to the end of the thirties in any film where glamorous dancing frocks were required. It was an enormously influential style.

It has never entered my mind to undertake to create theatrical costumes. I feel no inclination whatever to do so. There is, however, a type of dress destined to be worn and exhibited to the public which, while not coming under the heading of costume, is discernible by being more extravagant and conveying a hint of eccentricity non-existent in one of my ordinary gowns.

Patou understood that these dresses had to be entirely, yet only subtly, different from the ordinary evening gown in colour, cut and decorative ornamentation. Even in décolletage and length, they had to have their own rules. He set out to lay down the guidelines and was characteristically emphatic in his conclusions: 'The correct gown for the ballroom dancer should avoid entirely a stagey look,' he said, having understood perfectly that the appeal of this sort of performance was the idea that two 'ordinary' people just happened to get up and dance in a manner which, while it was extraordinary, looked so effortless that anyone could achieve it. 'What I dislike in any stage costume, however beautiful, is its lack of suppleness. This of course does not apply to character dancers.'

Blonde El Ambrose was, with her partner Maurice, one of the most famous of these dancers. Patou not only dressed her for her performances, but for her daytime life as well. It is fascinating to compare these clothes and their different design vocabularies, designed at exactly the same time for the same woman. For day, the ethereal Miss Ambrose wore clothes of typical quiet Patou subtlety, but for her professional appearances, the narrow *sportif* line was replaced by dresses designed to emphasize her suppleness, lightness and undulation.

'Anything likely to hinder movement and the rhythm of the dance – essential factors of such *danseuses* – is to be avoided. Every movement the dancer is likely to make should be emphasized by a corresponding fluttering of material,' said Patou.

'Dancing dresses I have made like this have been conceived along these general lines and are therefore always made of chiffon or tulle. Satins, or any such materials, through their very opaque qualities cannot be expected to give that impression of airy grace which dancers endeavour to convey.' He was very much in favour of ostrich feathers as a trimming but insisted that they be used with discretion.

Pursuing these ideas, Patou often shaded his tulle dancing dresses from light at the hem to dark at the waist and used less thicknesses of tulle at the hem than the waist. These technicalities, helped by strong upward stage lighting, contributed to the attractive, light appearance of the dancer, without, he believed, making it appear that she was wearing a costume. What Patou actually achieved was that feat of design legerdemain, the heightening of reality. Careful exaggeration, rethought proportion, a reversal of his normal rules were the secrets.

The major difference between these fantasy dresses and his other designs, however, was the distinct waistline which he often chose to emphasize with a glittering belt. 'The belt has no other object but that of outlining the slim grace of the artist for this, after all, is one of her absolutely essential requisites.'

The dance dresses, designed between 1924 and 1929, are crucial in considering Patou's development as a designer. Patou might otherwise have vanished with the demise of the *garçonne*. When the time finally came for fashion to alter, it was Patou who changed first, dramatically and definitively, not only by dropping hemlines, but by producing an entirely new silhouette. He had already been designing clothes which emphasized the waist and stressed flow and undulation. He had already worked on the correct proportions for the new look, so he was ready with a fully developed new design vocabulary.

The dresses, hybrids of fantasy and real-life clothes, gave Patou the means and the motivation to experiment with this different way of cutting clothes and dressing women and finally, with his winter 1929 collection, to kill off the *garçonne*. Patou was thus once again the first to perceive what women wanted and to dress them accordingly.

7

Patou's New Look

Perhaps once in a generation fashion responds to external stimuli and makes a major change in the whole look. Dior, in 1947, killed off the military, utilitarian tailored style that had lasted all through the forties. In 1962 Courrèges launched his space-age look, and the mini skirt was born.

In 1929, a similar kind of abrupt change occurred, and it was Patou who was generally conceded by contemporary fashion critics and journalists to have launched it. His change of tack seemed so sudden that it made international news, as well as electrifying those journalists whose business it was to report fashion.

By January 1930, *Vogue* were so confident of the continuance of this new, waisted, feminine, long look that they were able to make fun of it by publishing a very witty Beaton drawing, showing a group of *garçonne* women in the shortest of all possible skirts, and the same women, three months later, in long supple dresses. The gamin figure wearing a shapeless sack dress, with cropped hair, long dangling earrings, narrow strip diamond bracelets and the eternal bandeau had disappeared. The flat, straight look of the female body dressed in two-dimensional clothes was replaced suddenly not just by new clothes, but once again by a new body as well. A new ideal had been born. Long and curved, with a high but defined bust, and an exquisite back. Women were changing their shape and posture, it would seem from contemporary photographs, almost overnight.

The look caught on immediately. Fluid, becoming, it demanded the highest level of the dressmaker's art, for it was pieced together in basques and godets to create flow and drape to enhance the new, more rounded body. Instead of flat bosoms and long, stick-like legs, bare arms and bare backs, the new silhouette demanded a more womanly appearance. Concealment became fashionable, in direct contrast to the 'bare-all' policy of the *garçonne*. Chiffon fluttered over partly concealed legs, much collar detailing was shown, and faces were shaded by naughty little hats.

It was a major fashion revolution, comparable to the tidal wave created twenty years earlier by Poiret's oriental designs and it was Patou who fired the first salvo in what was to become a barrage. In his winter 1929 collection, he led off with a startling black and nasturtium yellow 'new look' dress, which developed the line he had toyed with that spring in a few evening dresses, and was now extending into every part of his collection. Other couturiers followed suit immediately.

Patou knew that times were changing and that clothes had to reflect the new spirit of subtlety and elegance. However certain he may have been that he was right, Patou nevertheless created his collection with the gravest misgivings. In a sense, in abandoning the *garçonne*, he was killing the golden goose that he himself had created. The night of his winter 1929 gala preview was the only time he was ever seen to suffer from an attack of appalling stage fright.

By the time the first mannequin had been approved in every detail and had walked on to the catwalk, Patou would usually have been in high spirits. Always excitable, collection night saw him at his best, keyed-up to receive the congratulations of smart Paris gathered beyond the curtain. He was so confident, normally, that he watched his collection from just behind the curtain.

This time it was different. The whole future of his couture house, and the business he and Raymond Barbas had painstakingly built up over the past ten years, was at stake. It was a magnificent gamble, worthy of the man who had also spent the last ten years losing fortunes at the baccarat and chemin de fer tables in the South of France.

Everything was staked on this one throw. Normally imperturbable, Patou showed uncharacteristic signs of nerves, and sent Georges Bernard, always at hand for any of his major projects, to stand in his usual place. Patou locked himself away in his office, and paced up and down in what was virtually a trophy room of the past ten years of success.

Ranged on the shelves were the perfume bottles, the beautiful Cartier lighters. He probably gazed at the portrait of his sister Madeleine, commissioned by him at the height of his success in 1925, and he worried. He told Bernard to come and tell him how it was being received the moment he had any reaction from the audience. He must have been very lonely for those few minutes in the quiet of the office.

At one with his thoughts, he waited to know whether the success and the business now employing nearly two thousand people would founder and vanish. Had his collection not been a success, he could have been ruined. There would be no second chance that season and, besides, there had already been sinister rumours from New York for those who cared to listen. Some American buyers, although in Paris in even greater numbers than they had been in the previous season, were looking worried.

About a quarter of the way through the collection, Bernard rushed back with the news. He had seen women in the front row, tugging ineffectually at their skirts, trying to cover their knees. They already felt *démodé*: Patou's great gamble had succeeded. The *garçonne* had been ordered to grow up.

Later, after the applause had died down and his books were fuller than they had been since the great 1925 success, he was to say that he had been inspired to create this new look by Chanel. This was no generous compliment, however; it was a stab in the back.

One day, so his carefully composed story went, he was at a tea party and saw some women sitting opposite him with Chanel skirts so short that he could see, as he put it, rather more than he felt was correct at that, or any other, time of the day. Inspired, he rushed back to his atelier and completely reworked his collection, using as a base the fluidly supple dresses he had been designing for stage dancers for the past three years.

It is a good story, but it could not have happened like that. Patou always commissioned special fabrics for every collection and these must have been put in hand nearly a year before the night of the August collection. For not only had hems lengthened and waists become defined, but the clothes themselves were made differently, and from different fabrics. All this took time to work out, and Patou spent longer on fittings than he had ever done when he was creating the *garçonne* dresses. Patou's new look was the result of shrewd foresight.

With one of its sudden reverses, fashion now banished the knee, erotic focus of the twenties, which now became invisible and unmentionable. It would not be seen again for ten years until, with the Second World War, militaristic fashion led to the stripped-for-action look.

The Hollywood studio heads were furious, for they had films which suddenly looked utterly out of date, starring such flappers as Joan Crawford and Clara Bow. But the fashionable world understood the new look, and they wore it as soon as Patou's workrooms could make the clothes.

'Legs seen from the front in the evening are, well, almost *démodé*,' said *Vogue*, that September, '. . . and all wrong unless seen under transparent chiffon or tulle. And real belts . . . bloused backs . . . fastenings, even, that hook up.' One gets the impression that they could scarcely believe what they were seeing. It was as if Patou had gone back to the days of truly *grande couture*, to Worth, Doucet and the Callot Soeurs. It was all perfectly in tune with what was to be the dominant mood of the thirties: retrospection.

'Here is the first dramatic change in dress that has occurred since the *garçonne* mode came in. Women are as womanly as ever they can be,' *Vogue* observed, confirming that the elegant androgyny so chic in the twenties had vanished. It would be thirty years before unisex fashion would return.

The change in fashion this year is almost wholly a change in proportion, the high belted waist, the long skirt which makes fashion dramatically, almost revolutionarily, new. The hips are more tightly gripped than ever and seem to go a long way down and a long way up. The feeling is of a long slim body. Patou's is the first collection visited. It is the time when the buyers from the world over are in Paris. They line the broad stairs at Patou, standing two by two until a *vendeuse* shall 'pass' each one. For Paris now has a black list of those buyers who come to buy just a dress or two and carry all of the others away in their mind's eye.

Vetting was particularly important with this collection, for those who could rush copies of the new look into shops all over America would make a great deal of money – and the house of Patou was making certain that most of the money would stay in its hands.

In the spring of 1929 Patou had experimented with a few evening dresses whose short hems dipped lower at the back, as a device to introduce his new look in a tentative manner and to gauge reaction. It had been successful, and it was typical of Patou to conduct a little unofficial market research in this way. He may have liked the idea of being called an inspired innovator, but in reality his inspiration was based on sound business principles. This is not to minimize the gamble he finally took. It is one thing to produce a few slightly longer evening dresses, quite another to project an entire collection upon a radically different silhouette.

Vogue reviewed the collection minutely, building up an iden-tikit picture of the new proportions and the new details.

First come the sports ensembles, consisting of one- or two-piece dresses with straight threequarter coats of figured jersey that have collars of beaver and fox. Many have crêpe-de-chine blousons worn over a skirt to match the tuck-in blouse of crêpe-de-chine, or over a marocaine dress.

In afternoon frocks the heightened waistline descends at the back and blouses slightly. Collars and cuffs, lingerie touches are on nearly everything. There is more black than anything, but Patou's new shade called 'Dark Dahlia' often replaces black. Afternoon shades are deep green and Patou's new deep copper red. Every dress follows the new line; it fits at the waist with long moulded hips and uneven pointed hems, sometimes touching the floor and even trailing on the ground.

An idea of the preparation that had gone into what Patou was describing as blind inspiration can be gained from a description of some of the fabrics he had developed with such stalwarts as Bianchini Ferier. *Fleur de soie*, for instance, was a completely new fabric, a *crêpe romain* with the weight of crêpe-de-chine, and some of the transparency of chiffon. In Patou's colours, too, he departed for ever from the cool, neutral twenties palettes, introducing dark subtle mixtures, of which 'Dark Dahlia', a red which was almost black, was one of the most original, and a cardinal crimson which printed lamés in red and gold, tulle in a deep purplish brown rather like black tulips, and velvets in subtle florals. These were

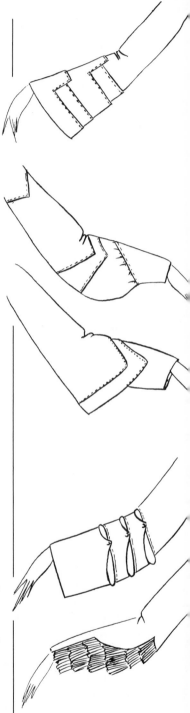

colours which had not been seen in the twenties. Black survived into the thirties, but it was always shown in softer, more textured fabrics, and as a ground to display small, brightly coloured flower prints.

The change was complete, and *Vogue* was definite about it.

What looked young last year looks old this season, all because longer fuller skirts and higher waistlines have been used so perfectly that they look right, smart and becoming. Which means there is now a new and less narrow way of being young and slim. There is a new length of line, in fact two, length of bodice and length of limb. . . . The new is, of course, in the minority but it is strong enough to leaven the whole fashion loaf very shortly.

A new flexibility of design was demonstrated in *Vogue*'s description of late afternoon dresses which 'go down to the ankles [and] seem to have one eye on the evening. It is only a short step from them to the informal evening dress. Afternoon dresses as a rule have long sleeves.'

A social observer writing diary notes for *Vogue* at this time said that conversation at Ritz teas suddenly turned from clothes and idle gossip to learned and scholarly subjects. As Patou said, 'That is probably the effect that long sleeves have on women's brains.' It was also the effect of the mood of the times for frivolity was fast vanishing in Paris in the last year of the decade, and it was time to turn to more serious matters.

The central point of this new look was the fact that these were serious clothes. 'Never has there been so much cut,' as *Vogue* put it.

Every type of dress is more intricate than it seems, or just as intricate as it looks. Line and pattern of fabric are used for all they are worth. That is why there is a feeling of mosaic or marquetry about many dresses. The variety that can be given an all-over print through different details is very great. Pleating, tucking, bias, horizontal or vertical bands, darts, hemstitching, bindings, pipings, all of these alter the design of any pattern.

There is a great deal of excitement in the air, and women sit and discuss the new developments, and they are a little uncertain of themselves. Even men discuss the new fashions. And those who have adopted them seem so happy that the rest are longing for the courage to follow.

By January 1930, *Vogue* were able to give readers a checklist of the new look:

Ten inches from the ground is the length for frocks at teatime in the home.

Our skirts will be clear to the ankle for restaurant dining and dancing.

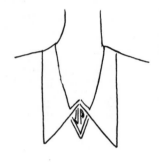

They will increase in length and go right down to the toes for a really grand occasion.

The waistline will refuse to move from its normal place in front, day or evening. However, it will sometimes slope to the back and slip out of sight under a bloused effect or under a lengthened bolero.

Bodices really tell the story of the future. In them lies the variety that is being relinquished by the long straight development of the skirt.

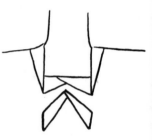

As bodices increase in importance, blouses will receive more and more attention and will be more in evidence; often they come out into the light of day as in a scarf collar or gilet on a suit.

It will be increasingly difficult to distinguish between a bodice and its neckline or to tell what its neckline treatment really is.

Décolletages will be softer and more varied than ever for both day and evening.

Bodices and blouses end in scarfs that are berthas [collars] that are jabots, jabots that are revers. They have surplice closings, they snap, they button and they tie low on the skirt rather than slipping simply over the head and tucking under the skirt.

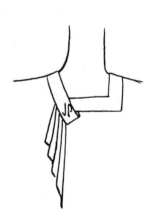

Bows will no longer be merely extraneous bits of decoration – untie your bow and you will be apt to lose your frock or your blouse.

The scarf as well is no longer a separate unit, but an increasingly integral part of the bodice.

Blouses and skirts are going to be on very good terms with each other. The blouse ties over the top of the skirt or else slips underneath, in which case a soft belt, attached to the top of the skirt, ties round the blouse.

Blouses will be charming in monochrome printed chiffons, self-patterned crêpe satins and muffler silks. Strict is a thing of the past.

This description, written in 1930, is a matrix for couture design for the rest of the decade (with the exception of the widened or exaggerated shoulder, introduced by Schiaparelli and Rochas simultaneously in 1932). Patou showed it complete in August 1929.

In creating the new look, Patou also created an evening 'uniform' that was to hold good until the mid-thirties: the bias-cut white satin evening dress. Women with pretensions to chic, such as Lady Colefax, and her arch-rival Syrie Maugham, adopted this way of dressing in the evening as a perfect counterpoint to the pale elegant interiors typical of the thirties.

Patou had already declared war against one clichéd classic and fired another salvo at his arch enemy: 'I shall fight with all my influence to banish the much too simple little black frock from the ranks of the fashionable,' he said in 1930, and the white satin slip, cut in triangular biased pieces was his answer: an evening uniform. Women loved it, and looked perfectly *au courant* as they lounged on banquettes at the Embassy Club in London or at '21' in New York.

But the real fight that Patou, together with the rest of the Paris couture, was about to face was not against the *garçonne* look or the little black dress. It was a great deal more serious and against a real enemy: the Depression. Couture was going to have to fight for its life in the face of the Wall Street crash of October 1929 and the severe depression that blighted the early thirties.

There was only the merest hint of trouble in Paris in the first half of 1929. The city lights blazed more brightly than ever. The number of foreign visitors was at its height and the couture business was working overtime, as were the many little ateliers that made trimmings, buttons and artificial flowers. The copyists on the rue de la Paix were also as busy as ever and the Ritz was packed to its rafters.

So brisk was business, so enormous the demand for clothes, that Patou and Lanvin opened their own ready-to-wear boutiques that year. Customers in a hurry could buy 'instant' couture that would need only minor alterations. These first ready-to-wear shops were an immediate success. The future seemed to stretch ahead of Patou and his colleagues in a pleasing vista of increased profits, and an ever-growing

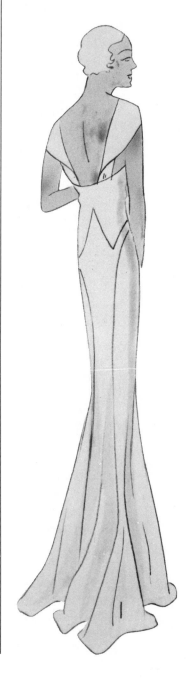

clientele. Perfume sales had surpassed even Patou's wildest hopes and, with the huge success of his new look, his future seemed assured. That summer, the Riviera season had been more brilliant than ever, and the summer couture house in Biarritz and the boutique in Deauville were working flat out.

But with the first cool days of autumn came the crash.

It is almost impossible, looking back over fifty years, to realize how total and how abrupt the fall was. Everything had changed. The future looked desperate, not only to those who had lost everything in the crash, but to anyone who had built up enormous industries founded on the money of the new rich, themselves created as a breed by the booming speculation of the twenties.

Trivial it may seem to discuss the disaster in couture terms, but couture employed huge numbers of people – not just in the Parisian houses, but throughout France, in textiles, in the perfume industry, in beading, in making shoes, in furs, jewels, buttons. Then there were the spinners, weavers, dyers, printers and embroiderers. It was a complex pyramid and by the end of the twenties the couture and its dependent concerns had become a large contributor to the overall French gross national product. Anything which threatened it became a threat to many French industries and affected even the humblest homes.

In January 1930 not one American buyer came to Paris. Private clients were still important in terms of creating publicity, but the amount of money even a Mrs Harrison Williams could spend on couture dressing in a year was dwarfed by the enormous sums paid by Seventh Avenue manufacturers for the right to copy. At one stroke, the industry was thrown back on its own resources with no immediate prospect of the situation improving. The prudent ones had saved and they reinvested a great proportion of their boom-time twenties earnings; those such as Patou, who were lucky enough to have established thriving spin-off businesses such as perfume, cosmetics and accessories, were not so hard hit.

Only one couture house closed during this period – Augustabernard. The rest put their workers, already fairly badly paid but accustomed to working long hours overtime, on part-time work, or laid them off, and struggled to survive with a dramatically reduced clientele. There were not many of them, as Janet Flanner, writing from Paris as Genet, in the *New Yorker*, reported in 1930:

The Wall Street Crash has had its effect here. In the rue de la Paix, the jewellers are reported to be losing fortunes in sudden cancellations of orders, and at the Ritz bar the pretty ladies are having to pay for their cocktails themselves. In the Quartier de l'Europe, little firms that live exclusively on the American trade have not sold one faked Chanel copy in a fortnight. A wholesale *antiquaire* in the Boulevarde Raspail has a cellar bulging with guaranteed Louis XIV candlesticks that are not moving.

Certain real estate advertisements were illuminating:

For sale, cheap, Nice Old Chateau, 1 hr. frm. Paris; Original Boiseries, 6 New Baths; Owner Forced Return New York Wednesday; MUST HAVE IMMEDIATE CASH; Will Sacrifice

Couture houses lived for a time on credit of one sort or another. They were given credit by the fabric houses against eventual sales, and they in turn extended credit to their better private and wholesale clients, and so it took about six months for the effect of the crash to show on their books.

Paradoxically, the private clientele had increased a little in the latter part of 1929. Stimulated by this total change in fashion, many women took the opportunity to renew their entire wardrobes, and this kept the couturiers busy until the early days of 1930. For a short while couture found itself busy becoming dressmakers in the old Worth manner once again. But, to survive, surplus fat was trimmed off ruthlessly. Appearances had to be kept up, however, for luxury was ultimately the heart of the success of Paris couture, and it was generally felt by Patou and his colleagues that a confident, even nonchalant, face must be presented to the world if couture was to weather the Depression.

Patou always came alive when danger threatened. He was lucky in that his house had always been well run financially, even though he had diverted a high proportion of the profits into gambling. That had not mattered during the

twenties when the profits and the design successes had seemed endless. But it was going to matter more in the thirties.

The crash stimulated Patou. It was exciting, and he responded immediately, with the instinct of a showman, by deciding to be more extravagant than ever. Early in 1930, he gave a magnificent party in the courtyard of his house in the rue de la Faisanderie. Janet Flanner reported, rather disapprovingly, in the *New Yorker*:

The most calculatedly dazzling of the soirées was given by the dressmaker Jean Patou. The guests being largely Italian, British and American, and the decorations silver. To obtain the desired effect, the garden was roofed over, and not only were the walls and low ceiling lined with silver foil, but also as much of the trees as were left visible, trunks, branches, even the twigs being wrapped in silver paper: and from the metal boughs hung silver cages as tall as a man, harboring overstuffed parrots as large as a child. One of the attractions was the Whispering Baritone, Jack Smith, who swept out after vainly whispering against the noise of illuminated fountains, electric ventilators and friendly guests, seated as at a night club, at different tables.

The second attraction was three small lion cubs, led in by lion-tamers in flowered shirts and imposing breeches; the cubs were then given as grab-bag prizes to guests who, as the story says, may not have wanted, but drew them.

Patou was not alone in such excesses. Throughout the thirties, fancy-dress balls became more and more elaborate, a glittering counterpoint to the grim economic situation. They were an escape into fantasy, and Patou designed many costumes for 'theme' balls in the early thirties. At a white ball given in Paris in 1932 by Cecil Pecci-Blunt, the American beauty Mrs John Monroe wore a beautiful Third Empire dress designed by Patou for her appearance as the Empress Eugénie. Among the court ladies who surrounded her in her tableau, all dressed in an *haut roman* style rather untypical of Patou, was the Baronne Albert de Goldschmidt Rothschild, in a full, stiffened, chiffon dress.

'Simplicity need not be poverty. Splendour is never bad taste. A beautiful gown may be simple, but should nevertheless give the impression of luxury.' Patou, at the beginning of the thirties, was still holding fast to his principles. He was beginning to become seriously isolated from the times. His gambling, his parties and his general recklessness were not only undermining his health, but were also distancing him from the pulse of things. He never really had any 'feel' for the thirties and after his last great success with his winter 1929 look he began – imperceptibly at first – to diverge from the mainstream of fashion innovation.

The mood of the times changed so suddenly, so radically, that many couturiers found it difficult to alter their thinking. Chanel, Lanvin and Patou, all great names in the twenties, found themselves flagging in the early thirties, elbowed out of the limelight by the sudden eminence of Schiaparelli, the volatile Italian artist who was very definitely part of the whole movement toward fantasy, surrealism and a rococo extravagance that marked the thirties. . . .

The effects of the First World War and of high living for a decade were catching up with Patou. Suave as ever, lines of worry can be detected nevertheless in his photographs. He looks as if he is trying just a little too hard, as if the laughter is forced and brittle, the smile not spontaneous.

After the last great triumph Patou's final years were sad ones. As the twenties faded from memory, and the *garçonne* became a type that authors like Nancy Mitford satirized with portraits such as that of Veronica Chaddesley Corbett in *Love in a Cold Climate*, so Patou faded too. He was a reminder of an era most people preferred to forget.

8

Shadows

By the winter of 1930, the number of foreigners visiting Paris twice a year for clothes dwindled almost to nothing as a result of the Depression, and the couture business was flung back on its original resources. These quietly elegant private European clients, such as Elsie de Wolfe and Mrs Harrison Williams, now became the backbone of the couture business once again, and this had an effect on fashion direction. Designs made to be widely copied must be relatively simple. Clothes for private clients, who are prepared to spend time having them fitted to perfection, and to their individual taste, however, can be much more complex.

Couture, in the early years of the thirties survived simply through much more complicated dressmaking. Two-dimensional simplicity – 'one size fits all' – had given way to elaborate, sinuous dresses cut in bias shapes, pieced together on the individual client. For day, immaculately fitted black suits, for night, backless sheaths of oyster or eau-de-nil satin. Precise, echoing the lines of the body, and needing several fittings to achieve the correct second-skin effect.

At first Patou was still buoyant. After all, women who could only afford one evening dress tended to choose the only possible one: Patou's white slipper satin, bias-cut sheath. Soon, every couturier had his or her version. It was usually cut in huge diamond shapes to follow the thirties ideal of a high rounded bust, long slim legs and a high waist. Patou had been designing for this shape for some time for the society wedding dresses he had specialized in since the beginning of the twenties, and although Vionnet has been rightly credited with inventing the bias cut, it was Patou who had worked out the classic sinuous sheaths.

As far back as 1924 he had created such a design for the wedding dress of Mlle Arrivabene who married Conte Visconti di Modrone in one of the grandest weddings Venice has seen this century. Patou was to amend the line, with variations, for wedding gowns which were simple enough to act as foils for priceless antique lace family veils. Smart society brides wore these classically simple dresses all the way through the twenties and into the thirties, culminating in the dress he designed for Barbara Hutton, for her wedding in 1933.

These white sheaths had powerful allies. Fashion photogaphers such as Hoyningen-Huene, who came into prominence at the end of the twenties, loved the simple sculptural lines which worked as a foil for the individuality of the beautiful society women he photographed for *Vogue*. Setting them in vaguely classical backgrounds, influenced by his travels in the Peloponnese, Hoyningen-Huene used the shining simplicity and fluidity of these dresses, echoing in their flowing lines the new proportion of the body. The artful touch of twisted halters, the precise placement of a lily, a popular prop at the time, or an asymmetric shoulder frill, made them marvellous props for the new style in fashion photography, which depended on mood created by lighting, dispensing with lifeless poses against flat backgrounds.

'Movement characterizes Patou's new gowns,' wrote *Harper's Bazaar* in 1931, 'and the dresses echo every move of their wearer.' Patou and Vionnet had each managed to achieve apparent simplicity in these *rien* dresses, but they were really extremely sophisticated examples of the dressmaker's art, and customers such as Gertrude Lawrence, Lady Colefax and many other arbiters of elegance at the beginning of the thirties popularized them as the smartest look for evening.

By 1932, the mood was imperceptibly shifting as the rich recovered from the Wall Street crash and fashionable life got into its stride again. Taste was changing and painters, fashion photographers and interior decorators were to be important architects of this change, from the neat, cubist-inspired mode of the twenties, to the rococo extravagances of the thirties.

It was a wicked, gossipy, homosexual world that began to establish itself as a profound influence on Paris social life in general, and fashion and other applied arts in particular – a milieu from which Patou, now in his fifties, found himself increasingly isolated. What could this middle-aged man of giddier times have had in common with leaders of the new milieu such as Cocteau? Not much – and it began to show.

One important group did little to help Patou's career in the thirties, and these were the fashion photographers who had just recently begun to wield an influence on what went into the important editorial pages. Photographers in the vanguard of this movement had never exerted real influence during the twenties, as had the illustrators such as André Marty or Georges Lepape. They were usually considered a necessary evil if one wanted a record of a gown, or a bland advertising portrait of some personality prepared to endorse clothes. They were sometimes thought of as an amusing, if ephemeral, innovation. The two leaders, Baron Gayne de Meyer and Edward Steichen, working for *Harper's Bazaar* and *Vogue* respectively at the end of the twenties, were the only two who really wielded any power. Steichen was reclusive and was influential simply because he took beautiful photographs. Baron de Meyer, on the other hand, was more involved in the social life that went with fashion and, indeed, quite often in the late twenties wrote about what smart people were wearing at parties he had attended.

The influence in fashion magazines of twenties illustrators, however, such as Bébé Bérard, 'Faceless Freddie' as Beaton affectionately called him, or Willaumez, or Eric, all of whose personal taste in fashion, decor and even in colour affected the way people wanted to look, was partly the result of the primitive stage of blockmaking: if an editor wanted colour, she was forced to use a fashion illustration rather than a photograph.

As the thirties progressed, fashion magazines began to use photographs more and more. The tiny halftones of the beginning of the decade grew to double-page spreads. A whole new generation of fashion photographers, with a point of view about the clothes they photographed and their appropriate environments, emerged, and they were to wield enormous power from then on.

Perhaps the two most accomplished of this first generation of internationally recognized fashion photographers (who included Man Ray, Munkacsi, André Durst, Erwin Blumenfeld,

Louise Dahl-Wolfe, and Horst), were Georges Hoyningen-Huene and Cecil Beaton, who combined fashion photography with portraiture, illustration and the writing of society tittle-tattle. They were both perfectly in tune with the spirit of the new decade and both exerted a considerable influence on the status and degree of publicity accorded to any couturier.

Beaton represented what he later described as:

the generally prevailing recklessness of style. My pictures became more and more rococo and surrealist. Society women as well as mannequins were photographed in the most flamboyant Greek-tragedy poses, in ecstatic or highly mystical states, sometimes with the melodramatic air of a Lady Macbeth caught up in a cocoon of tulle. Like the souls in torment seen in Hieronymous Bosch's hell, ladies of the upper crust were to be seen in *Vogue* photographs breaking their way out of a hat box, or breaking through a huge sheet of white paper or torn screen, as though emerging from a nightmare.

Princesses were posed trying frantically to be seen through a plate-glass window that had been daubed with whitewash.

In fact, white [said Beaton] was the one regular keynote of these proceedings. White-on-white paper was often used as a background, with a woman in white holding a sheaf of whitened branches in front of it. Perfectly normal ladies were pictured in extremes of terror with one arm covering the face or thrust forward in exaggerated perspective straight toward the camera.

Backgrounds were equally exaggerated and often tasteless. Badly carved cupids from junk shops on Third Avenue would be wrapped in argentine cloth or cellophane. Driftwood was supposed to bring an air of neo-romanticism to a matter-of-fact subject.

This 'recklessness' extended to decoration, which also exerted a profound influence on fashion throughout the thirties. 'Night clubs were done up as bird cages,' said Beaton, describing them as 'baroque excesses in plasterwork allied to the plush luxuries of late Victorianism'. Sugary colours, magentas, pinks, together with bright yellows, were favourites and, of course, Syrie Maugham's white-on-white decorations featuring priceless Louis XIV *bergères* stripped in acid to a uniform ash-beige were perfectly in tune with the generally crazy atmosphere. Little wonder that Patou, the aesthete, found himself increasingly out of sympathy with the mood.

Art, as well as interior decoration and photography, was a major fashion influence in the thirties. Dali's cooperation with Schiaparelli dressed women in surreal sweaters and leg-of-lamb felt hats. Picasso's *fausse pauvre* women – the well-fed rich playing at being ill-fed and poor – engendered a flurry of imitative fashion photography featuring smartly dressed society women posing against 'scabrous walls in Brooklyn', as Beaton put it. Even the anti-fashion painter Tchelitchew made a mark, if in a roundabout way. When his decor and costumes for Giraudoux's ballet *Ondine* were unveiled, an instant vogue was created for fish nets, stalactites, coral branches and driftwood. Beaton observed plaintively that fish nets looked rather strange draped across the staircase of a Wiltshire mansion.

Apart from the photographers, painters and decorators, a handful of chic couture clients also exerted the sort of influence on fashion that had not rested in the hands of individuals since the days of the Empress Eugénie. Velvet-gloved they may have looked, but their iron grip on the taste of fashionable society strengthened as the decade went on. There were two groups, the triumvirate *les dames de Vogue* and the rival group *les dames de Fémina*. The latter group, linked with the magazine *Fémina*, were much less important, their power generally confined to Paris alone. In a sense the two groups usurped the couturier's traditional role as a leader of fashionable taste. This was something Patou had great difficulty in understanding – and no doubt little sympathy.

Les dames de Vogue were by far the more influential, a reflection of the power of the magazine in which they appeared constantly during the thirties. The triumvirate was composed of Marie-Laure de Noailles, the poet and patron of the arts, Princess Nathalie Paley, who represented beauty and allure and who had at one point been married to the couturier Lucien Lelong, and 'Baba' de Faucigny-Lucinge, born Baba d'Erlanger, who concerned herself with being ahead of fashion.

Their taste, their clothes, their jewels and their interior decoration were all copied by *Vogue* readers, and fashion designers heeded their opinions. The thirties, through these women and others such as Mrs Reginald Fellowes, developed into an era when personal style was more important than mass fashion. The individual expression of style from *les dames de Vogue* set the mode for many and often with disastrous results, for what might suit Marie-Laure de Noailles, Daisy Fellowes or Lilia Ralli, one of Lelong's most devoted customers, did not suit all women, as much because these individualists brought a touch of personal fantasy and whimsy to anything.

Daisy Fellowes, for instance, would be seen wearing Jean Schlumberger's naturalistic diamond leaves, to which she had wittily pinned a fresh flower. She was a favoured customer of Schiaparelli and, although her Singer millions did not make economy necessary, she enjoyed the publicity of being dressed by 'Schiap' *à l'oeil*, in other words, for free.

This then was the new era which greeted Patou. A time of individual style, of fantasy, of the return of the private customer to a position of influence in couture, and an era when applied art and fashion intermingled. Personal style was all, and a small number of stylish women dominated couture. Patou never really appreciated that enormously influential socialites had consigned him to the past in favour of the wittier, more fantastic ideas of Schiaparelli.

To Patou, who had created his business based on the idea that many different types of women would be able to wear his clothes and would follow his lead, the thirties were soon to prove disastrous. Between 1929, a very successful year, and 1932, the problem was not apparent. Patou had coasted along happily making elegant longer-skirted day suits, often with fur collars, and his slipper satin evening dresses proved successful too. He had followed the general fashion in creating witty little hats, and though fashion had moved away from the sports look for everyday life, sports clothes for active sports were still a profitable part of his business. He was a follower, not a leader, in these later years.

The turning point came with the winter collection of 1932. Patou decided that the time had come, as a leading couturier, to launch another major fashion look, and, for the first time in his career, he got the timing and indeed the style totally wrong.

What induced him to move away from his principles of

simplicity and sinuous bias cutting, producing the character-istically thirties narrow-hipped elongated silhouette, is any-body's guess. But in a characteristic all-or-nothing gesture, similar to the one he made when he dropped hemlines in 1929, he abandoned these proportions in favour of a medieval revival, an extraordinarily heavy look with much emphasis upon the hips. He dropped the waists of his dresses to the hips, cutting pointed or diamond-shaped hemlines, from which he twisted and draped heavy panels of fabric. Ruching and draping around the hips created a stolid, almost preg-nant, look, reminiscent of his work in the early twenties, before he had developed his line.

This was not a whim on Patou's part. In the Patou archives for 1932 there are three boxes of reference drawings of me-dieval clothes, accessories and hats, clearly taken from such sources as the Duc de Berri's *Book of Hours*, and from medieval paintings: page after page of heavy pointed sleeves, of girdles, of square, fur-trimmed necklines speak for themselves. This collection was a considered decision on Patou's part.

Some of the dresses were bi- and tricoloured and panels were twisted, then embroidered in medieval motifs, or ruffled, all of which added to the heaviness and dullness of the look, and they were often amplified by trailing medieval sleeves, also edged in fur. A variation was called the 'bluebell' look, and here again the waist was dropped, but the skirts were fuller, sometimes even bell-shaped, enlarging the hips still further. These clothes made women look as matriarchal as they had in medieval paintings. Quite simply, Patou had got the erogenous zone wrong.

James Laver in *Style and Fashion* suggests that every era of fashion creates its own special erogenous zone. In the twen-ties, it was legs. In the thirties, it was not the stomach and the hips, as it had been in medieval times, it was the back. Every truly fashionable mid-thirties dress is slim and narrow, with wider shoulders, tiny hips, and the design interest con-fined to the back. Often bare to the waist in the evening, sometimes even in the daytime, demure afternoon dresses were likely to be slit to the waist at the back. Towards the middle of the thirties bustle effects began to appear, while the front of the dress or the suit was perfectly plain.

Patou's look was totally out of touch with the times: it was a disaster from which he never recovered. In the context of the twenties, when fashion pronouncements by couturiers were slavishly followed by the mass market they had created, it might – just – have worked. But in the individually stylish thirties, this unattractive new 'uniform' was ignored.

The two rising stars of the Paris couture, Schiaparelli and Lelong, were producing very different clothes. Schiaparelli, the volatile Italian 'artist turned dressmaker', as Chanel derisively described her, had launched the wider shoulder which she padded, epauletted, embroidered, even feathered, to increase the width. The rest of her silhouette was snake thin and the overall effect was one of absolute, dramatic, sometimes even ugly, chic. Daisy Fellowes, a favourite Schiaparelli customer, created a sensation at the Paris Opéra when she arrived in Schiaparelli's black broadcloth dinner suit with huge shoulders, exaggerated still further by black aigrette feathers.

It was not matriarchal, it was not even feminine – in fact it was rather masculine – but the new look was somehow chic. It was made more feminine by little nonsense hats from Schiaparelli, Regnier, Reboux or Suzanne. In fact, if thirties fashion could be summed up in one word, it would be 'hat'.

Lucien Lelong, the other star of thirties Paris couture, represented a more romantic aspect. He specialized in creating the simplest, wispiest clothes in pretty flowing fabrics and his perfect model was his wife, Princess Nathalie Paley, the pale blonde half-sister of Patou's old flame, the Grand Duchess Marie of Russia. Nathalie Paley's ethereal fairness set off Lelong's clothes to perfection, creating romantic neoclassic overtones of Greek statues on the move. One of the leading *dames de Vogue*, Princess Nathalie made sure that she was always photographed in her husband's clothes.

The Schiaparelli hard-edged chic with its witty surrealist overtones and Lelong's romantic neoclassic simplicity were the Scylla and Charybdis of fashion looks between which Patou's lumpish medievalism was crushed. It was far removed from the pulse of the times.

Chanel, too, had had her wings clipped by Schiaparelli, who had set up a rival fashion-social salon with a court of surrealist painters, fashion photographers and important fashion editors such as the young Diana Vreeland, who wore

130

her clothes. Chanel suffered as a consequence. Her clothes became 'pretty' and during this period stray from her deepest convictions towards an unfortunate artifice.

It is immediately noticeable from contemporary fashion magazines that Patou was suddenly demoted in favour of the new stars. Where he would always have been assured of important editorial comment before 1932, he was treated almost as an afterthought in issues between 1932 and 1936, playing at most second fiddle to Schiaparelli, whose clothes and hats then dominated the pages. Vionnet, who had a glittering list of *les dames de Vogue* as private clients, notably Mona Harrison Williams and another fashion leader, the exquisite Madame Martinez de Hoz, was secure. Patou hats are shown, the occasional suit, some evening dresses, and that is all.

The years 1932 to 1935 must have anguished Patou for he no doubt felt that the spirit of the times, once the very atmosphere he breathed, was now air that choked him. His health, never a problem before, began rapidly to deteriorate. The decade and a half of high living, hard work and high jinks, as well as the war hardships, appeared to have undermined his constitution, causing him to age quickly. Photographs taken at the time show a man looking years older than he should. Raymond Barbas gradually found himself in control of more and more of the business.

Patou's diversions into other markets helped, for many of the innovations he had introduced in the twenties tided the business over these lean times. His perfumes continued to sell well and steadily as did *les riens*. Money was much tighter for most couturiers – Patou, however, ignored the economic climate which, though improved since 1929, was still sombre.

He gambled more extravagantly than ever, but he could no longer sell as many evening dresses to make up his losses as he used to, for even the wealthiest women were buying fewer outfits per season, while the wholesalers were beginning to follow the new couture stars. Patou's business now relied more and more on making quietly distinguished clothes for a group of faithful, discriminating private clients. There was little hope of the couture business once again assuming an all-powerful role. A younger generation spoke a new language, and even though some of his new clothes revealed his sureness

Un PERFUME
JEAN PATOU
París

es siempre un perfume
distinguido

Ultima supercreación
JEAN PATOU
París

JOY

El aristócrata entre los perfumes más
finos del mundo. Es tan vibrante y
concentrado, que una sola gota hará
las delicias de muchas tardes.

Otras grandes
creaciones

AMOUR AMOUR
MOMENT SUPREME
INVITATION
VACANCES
NORMANDIE

PARIS: 9, Rue Saint-Florentin (8°)
NEW YORK: 730 Fifth Avenue

De venta en las buenas perfumerías

DISTRIBUIDOR GENERAL PARA ESPAÑA:

R. J. ARAGONÉS

BARCELONA: Casanova, 75
MADRID: San Bernardo 120

of touch, they did not speak the language of the times. To the correctly and quietly dressed Parisian and foreign clients such as the elegant Jean de Noailles, Patou was still an important source of beautifully fitted, correctly elegant clothes. But to those freer thirties spirits, Patou had become yesterday's news.

Towards the end of 1934, however, it seemed that Patou was about to enjoy a modest Indian summer. After the medieval collection, which had met with little response from the American retailers, Patou never aimed at changing fashion. He began to follow the new leaders and this in itself was demoralizing to him. He may have reflected on the fate of couturiers who did not move with the times, such as Paul Poiret, now being supported by handouts from friends and former colleagues and living in penury in the city he had ruled as king of fashion for so long. The same could happen to Patou.

Looking at the few magazine illustrations of 1935 and 1936, it can be seen that Patou was, nevertheless, fighting back — and finally more in step with the thirties. He produced a group of zebra-printed evening dresses that started a craze for this black and white print, which ended up on the famous banquettes in the New York night club, El Morocco.

He was beginning to develop a new line, inspired by *fin-de-siècle* bustles and draping. Flirting with the wider shoulder, he puffed it into a soft leg-of-mutton sleeve, and produced a wonderful series of hourglass-shaped, dulled satin evening dresses with very marked waists, tight bodices and huge bowed and bustled backs, which were balanced by tiny evening hats.

The bustles of Patou's gowns grew into trains, either full and flowing or fish tail, to emphasize this new curved silhouette. For a while, the magazines began to take notice of his work again, and in the spring and winter of 1935 we find more space devoted to these newly accomplished Patou dresses.

Fashion leaders such as Millicent Rogers wandered back to the rue St Florentin again, and, once there, they appreciated Patou's unerring standard of workmanship. But she is reported as having been at a dance at the Ritz, New York, late in 1935, where she kept changing her dress, abandoning

her Patou black silk gown with bustle and train on the pretext of having sat on some ice cream, for instance. While Schiaparelli was dramatic, her ideas daring and original, her workmanship was not so good, and some of the strange fabrics she translated into startling clothes could not even withstand drycleaning. Diana Vreeland, editor then of *Harper's Bazaar* and a great Schiaparelli fan, sent one of her Schiaparelli dresses to the cleaners and the next day was told that there was nothing left of it: it had dissolved in the solvent.

The reaction against 'instant' fashion set the stage for Patou's success with his well-made cothes. This mild change of fortune at the age of fifty-seven simply came too late. Worn out with fatigue, anxiety, and compensating with ever more frenetic gambling, he proved unequal to the tremendous demands he always made upon himself.

In 1936, he died quite suddenly, just after he had shown his spring collection. The official announcement was that he had died from an apoplectic fit. He died in relative obscurity in Paris and virtually bankrupt. 'He died because he was worn-out,' says Raymond Barbas. 'The First World War finally killed him.' Whatever the reason for his demise may have been physically, his mental state must have been an important contributing factor. Disappointment and disillusion do not kill directly.

His friends Louis Sue and André Mare, as devoted companions through the failures of the thirties as the successes of the twenties, paid him one final compliment: they designed his tomb, and he lies buried under a simple, beautiful monument, not just to a man, but also to the spirit of the age in which he had found success and fame.

Patou had had a splendid career. He had seen the couture business change from providing handmade clothes for a pampered elite, to an industry which influenced women all over the world.

His spirit and perception of changing social mores in the twenties had ensured him a place as a leader among his contemporaries. People who knew what exquisite design could be, who understood the subtle compliment a Patou dress paid to their personality, had bought their clothes from him.

The final irony of his life was that he died before he had a chance to make an effective comeback. He had always trusted to luck, and it would seem that it was returning, for at the end of his life he seemed to have recovered some sureness of touch and elegance of line. Perhaps he had finally come to terms with the thirties. The world of fashion has tended to ignore him, and he has been dismissed by many as a couturier who flourished only briefly in the twenties.

The results of his tireless search to achieve new results, his understanding of what the independent twentieth-century woman wants to look like can be seen today in every store that sells sweaters and skirts. The concept of active sportswear as an influence on fashion, never so popular as it is at the moment, was virtually invented by Patou and his best model, Suzanne Lenglen.

His monument is our freedom to wear comfortable, stylish sports clothes. If he had continued creating these wonderful looks, 'Patou' might have become a style rather than a fashion anchored to its time. Style is permanent and timeless, fashion is ephemeral – and Patou was always more concerned with fashion, with the moment and the mood, than he was with timelessness.

Epilogue

When he died in 1936, Patou left two guardians who continued the business that he had created and almost destroyed. They built it up again, basing it on the tradition of superb workmanship that Patou had established when he started in 1919, and which he had never abandoned. His sister Madeleine and Raymond Barbas had both been imbued with Patou's sense of elegance and timing. They determined to carry on the business although the central figure had died.

A measure of their success can be understood when one realizes that Patou is the only couture house, with the exception of Lanvin, which flourished in the twenties and which is still wholly owned by direct descendants of the original founder. Other names have come, gone, or been taken over by conglomerates, but the house of Patou continues.

The salons are just as they were when Patou had them decorated by Sue and Mare. You can still walk through the interlocking studios and find fabric swatches pinned on the wall in preparation for the next couture collection. The heady smell of Joy wafts up the marble staircase and there are still private customers having fittings in the wooden *cabines*, as their grandmothers did before them.

Up at the top of the house, there are still the long worktables, scattered with pieces of *toile* and pins. The couture business may have its ups and downs but Patou left more than a name. He left a business that has flourished and the perfumes too, which have grown into a business so vast that even he would have been astonished.

Raymond Barbas has always had a good eye for design talent. He has employed, among others, Christian Dior, who used to sell him sketches in the thirties, Gérard Pipart, now of

Nina Ricci, Michel Goma, Marc Bohan and Karl Lagerfeld, who by some irony has now become the designer at Chanel. It is as if the spirit of Patou, perhaps standing in some window embrasure, hovering over the fabrics in the studio, pervades the whole house, nearly fifty years after his death.

Patou's concepts have spread to a completely new generation of designers who look again at his sports-influenced designs of the twenties. The cubist sweaters are from time to time revived, particularly in Italy, and his sweater-and-skirt combination crops up every season in one form or another.

There are few Patou clothes in costume collections, perhaps because their original owners wore them out, but also because Jean Patou has been consistently underestimated by fashion historians. Wedding dresses, because worn only once, survive in the Metropolitan Museum in New York. There are evening clothes in the Brighton Museum of Costume, and in the Centre de la Documentation de la Couture Française in Paris. The most valuable sources of information are the archives at the couture house itself. Year by year, season by season, the sketches of the finished collections, executed by many hands, are filed; so are photographs of the clients, and many record photographs of the clothes themselves.

Raymond Barbas has maintained a remarkable consistency of style over the years. Every designer who has worked for Patou has produced clothes which in some sense echo Patou in his great days.

Jean Patou was lucky with his family's strict adherence to his guiding principles. In their guardianship of his reputation they have made sure that the name 'Patou' still stands for quality. Jean de Mouy, now president of the company, is already carrying the business into a third generation. The house of Patou survives and is firmly built on those few inspirational years that spanned the 1920s.

The world of Hispano Suizas, green cloche hats, cubist sweaters and tea at the Ritz has vanished for ever. But the name of the man who was one of the few to understand the mood of the first really modern decade of the twentieth century survives. Every time a woman buys a bottle of Joy, every time a striped V-necked sweater is pulled down over a pleated skirt, every time real sports clothes are used as an inspiration for fashion design, Patou survives. It is no bad legacy.

Bibliography

Antoine, *Antoine by Antoine*, Prentice-Hall, 1945

Arlen, Michael, *The Green Hat*, Collins, 1924

Ballard, Bettina, *In My Fashion*, David McKay Co., 1960

Battersby, Martin, *The Decorative 20s*, Studio Vista, 1969

Batterberry, Michael and Ariane, *A Social History of Fashion*, Holt, Rinehart & Winston, 1977

Beaton, Cecil, *The Glass of Fashion*, Weidenfeld & Nicolson, 1954

Beaton, Cecil, *Selected Diaries, 1926–1974*, Weidenfeld & Nicolson, 1979

Belle, Jean-Michel, *Les Folles Années de Maurice Sachs*, Grasset, 1979

Brunhammer, Yvonne, *Lo Stile 1925*, Fratelli Fabbri Editore, 1966

Charles-Roux, Edmonde, *Chanel*, Grasset, 1979

Daves, Jessica, *Ready-Made Miracle*, G. P. Putnam's Sons, 1967

De Wolfe, Elsie, *After All*, Heinemann, 1935

Flanner, Janet, *Paris Was Yesterday*, ed. I. Drutman, Viking, 1973

Garland, Madge, *The Indecisive Decade*, Macdonald, 1968

Haney, Lynn, *Naked at the Feast*, Robson Books, 1981

Howell, Georgina, *In Vogue*, Allen Lane, 1975

Lardner, John, *The Aspirin Age, 1919–1941*, Penguin Books

Laver, James, *Between the Wars*, Vista Books, 1961

Laver, James, *The Jazz Age*, Hamish Hamilton, 1964

Lynham, Ruth (ed.), *Paris Fashion*, Michael Joseph, 1972

Marguerite, Victor, *La Garçonne*, Gallimard, 1923

Poiret, Paul, *En Habillant l'Epoque*, Grasset, 1930

Sachs, Maurice, *La Décade de l'Illusion*, Gallimard, 1932

Woolman Chase, Edna, *Always in Vogue*, 1954

Yoxall, H. W., *A Fashion of Life*, Heinemann, 1966

Magazines

Gazette du Bon Ton – Art, modes frivolités, published by the Librairie Centrale des Beaux-Arts from 1913 to 1915; published by Condé Nast from 1920 to 1925

Vogue, New York, Paris, London, published by Condé Nast

Harper's Bazaar, New York, London, published by Hearst

Index